Medieval Cityscapes Today

PAST IMPERFECT

Past Imperfect presents concise critical overviews of the latest research by the world's leading scholars. Subjects cross the full range of fields in the period ca. 400—1500 CE which, in a European context, is known as the Middle Ages. Anyone interested in this period will be enthralled and enlightened by these overviews, written in provocative but accessible language. These affordable paperbacks prove that the era still retains a powerful resonance and impact throughout the world today.

Director and Editor-in-Chief

Simon Forde, *'s-Hertogenbosch*

Production

Ruth Kennedy, *Adelaide*

Cover Design

Martine Maguire-Weltecke, *Dublin*

Medieval Cityscapes Today

Catherine A. M. Clarke

British Library Cataloguing in Publication Data
A catalogue record for this book is available from the British Library

ISBN (print): 9781641891127
e-ISBN (PDF): 9781641891134
e-ISBN (EPUB): 9781641891141

www.arc-humanities.org
Printed and bound by CPI Group (UK) Ltd, Croydon, CR0 4YY

Contents

List of Illustrations

For Thomas, a fellow explorer

Preface

This book uses new research to investigate the scholarly understanding, heritage management, and public interpretation of medieval cityscapes today. Drawing on two contrasting central case studies, it asks questions about approaches to medieval cityscapes in very different forms and contexts: where rich material survivals are still present in the urban landscape, associated with an established culture of heritage tourism; and where the medieval urban environment is absent or invisible today. What research methods can scholars use to explore the medieval cityscape, in its varying forms? And what tools and techniques can enable us to engage wider communities with medieval cityscapes today?

Emerging technologies and expanding digital possibilities make these questions particularly timely and urgent today. New immersive technologies, augmented reality, and virtual historic environments are collapsing the established models and discourses of heritage research and practice, challenging us to think about place and the past in new ways. Where scholars and practitioners have relied on categories such as those of "tangible" and "intangible" heritage, new technologies instead posit an incipient, hybrid realm which merges the material, cultural, and imagined. What constitutes the medieval cityscape today? Is it a material phenomenon or can it be a virtual world? Is it a space of history, reality, or conceptual play? This book takes new technologies as a provocation to ask fundamental questions about how we should now understand and define historic environments in a digital age.

As well as confronting the implications of digital tools and technologies, this book also examines creative practice as a mode both for public interpretation, and for scholarly inquiry and exploration. The case studies at the core of this volume incorporate experimental, creative initiatives alongside traditional scholarly research methods in their engagement with medieval urban environments. How can projects such as a civic art commission, or development of a computer game enhance public understanding of the medieval cityscape today? And how can these approaches enlarge academic practice and prompt new questions or insights?

The mission of the "Past Imperfect" series ideally supports the aims of this study. *Medieval Cityscapes Today* addresses scholars across a range of disciplines—from history to archaeology to heritage science—as well as professionals in the heritage sector, creative practitioners, policy-makers, and others who are responsible for the conservation and development of our urban spaces. It seeks to make research-led provocations and prompts to new thinking and practice across both scholarship and applied heritage management.

Most of all, though, this book seeks to address fellow academics, and to offer a manifesto for the ways in which new—or more flexible, more capacious—research methods and ways of working might allow Humanities scholars to assert more of a stake in contemporary urban life and the formation of our shared public realm. Thinking critically about the ways in which we mutually police the limits of our disciplines and authority—and the ways in which we could challenge these boundaries—potentially opens up new spaces for scholars from a wide range of subject backgrounds to make interventions in the management and interpretation of historic urban environments today.

Acknowledgements

This book builds on collaborative research funded by the UK Arts and Humanities Research Council. The team for "Mapping Medieval Chester" (2008–2009) included Keith Lilley (Queen's University Belfast) and Helen Fulton (now University of Bristol) as Co-Investigators, with Mark Faulkner (Trinity College Dublin) as Post-Doctoral Researcher. The project "Discover Medieval Chester" also involved Keith Lilley, and a team at the Grosvenor Museum, Chester, led by Susan Hughes. "City Witness: Place and Perspective in Medieval Swansea" included Keith Lilley and Paul Vetch (then Department of Digital Humanities, King's College London) as Co-Investigators, and Gareth Dean and Harriett Webster as Post-Doctoral Researchers.

Moving on from these projects, the research for this book has benefited from the questions, comments, and ideas of many colleagues, including participants at the Medieval Research Seminar in the Faculty of English Language and Literature, University of Oxford and the MEMORI medieval research seminar at Cardiff University. Invitations to give the keynote lecture at the 2014 Digital Heritage conference (University of York), the 2016 Denys Hay Lecture (University of Edinburgh) and a plenary lecture at the 2016 "Lost and Transformed Cities: A Digital Perspective" conference (Lisbon) also all gave me opportunities to develop research for this book and to learn from other current work in the field.

I would also like to offer personal thanks to Leonie Hicks, John McGavin, and, especially, Keith Lilley, for their generous help and advice. Finally, I wish to thank my former colleagues in the Department of English, University of Southampton, where I researched and completed this book: in gratitude for all your support, inspiration, and friendship.

Notes

While the title of this book is very broad, I have chosen to focus on case-study towns and cities in western Europe, and mostly in the United Kingdom. This choice reflects my own scholarly interests, expertise, and personal experience: I acknowledge the limits of my focus here and that a different geographical and cultural range would bring varying issues and questions into the foreground. Nonetheless, I hope my arguments and insights here apply to many towns and cities, especially across Europe, and that they can contribute to wider debates about heritage in a global context today.

In order to keep footnotes to a minimum, subsequent citations of sources are usually referenced in brackets in the main text. Key background sources and "Further Reading" are given at the end of the book.

Rouen: Introduction

I'm standing high on the Cathedral of Notre Dame, looking down over the medieval cityscape of Rouen, Normandy. It is late May, 1431: trees blossom in gardens, the fields across the Seine are lush and green, ships cluster either side of the Pont Mathilde, where cargo is hauled up the riverbanks. I can see the Abbey of Saint Ouen, caged in wooden scaffolding, where the tower and nave are under construction. To the north, I see the squat, round towers of Rouen Castle, with the crenellations of the city wall behind them; towards the west, near the river, the English are hard at work on their new fortress—later to be known as the Vieux Palais. Smoke drifts up from handsome, four-storey timbered houses in the Rue Grand-Pont, where a small crowd has gathered to watch a group of masked entertainers perform in the street. I can hear the chatter of children playing in the Cour d'Albane cloister below me, bells chiming in the distance, the ring of masons' tools as they work the new Gothic arches at the top of the Saint Romain tower.

Taking in this panoramic view of the city, I recall the startling description of Rouen in the twelfth-century *Ecclesiastical History* of Orderic Vitalis. After a local revolt against Robert, Duke of Normandy, in 1090, the rebel leader Conan is taken to the top of the ducal tower by Robert's brother Henry (the future Henry I of England), to be shown the wealth and beauty of the city which he has coveted.

Considera Conane, quam pulchram tibi conatus es subicere. En ad meridiem delectabile parcum patet oculis tuis; et saltuosa regio siluestribus abundans feris. Ecce Sequana piscosum flumen Rotomagensem murum allambit; nauesque pluribus mercimoniis refertas huc cotidie deuehit. En ex alia parte ciuitas populosa minibus sacrisque templis et urbanis edibus speciose; cui iure a priscis temporibus subiacet Normannia tota.

Regard, Conan, the beauty of the country you tried to subordinate. See to the south before your eyes lies a delightful park, wooded and well-stocked with beasts of the chase. See how the river Seine, full of fishes, laps the wall of Rouen and daily brings in ships laden with merchandise of many kinds. See on the other side the fair and populous city, with its ramparts and churches and town buildings, which has rightly been the capital of Normandy from the earliest days.[1]

Henry's speech taunts Conan with the conventions of medieval urban encomium (praise of a city), before the traitor is flung from the tower to his death. Orderic's text presents the fantasy of a city fully seen, comprehended, enjoyed, and possessed: the Latin itself puns on the seductive, dangerous imaginative slippage between beholding and holding—ruling—the delightful landscape laid out below ("tibi conatus es *subicere*" / "*subiacet* Normannia tota"). For modern readers, this fantasized version of the city in its totality must also recall Michel De Certeau's seminal discussion of the view over New York from the World Trade Center towers and the "erotics of knowledge" which he associates with this elevated perspective on the urban landscape. De Certeau reflects on "this pleasure of 'seeing the whole', of looking down on, totalizing the most immoderate of human texts"—the city itself—which simultaneously disconnects and distances the viewer from the "ordinary practitioners of the city" who make its multiple, intersecting, illegible meanings, deep in the streets below.[2]

So, how have I come to be looking down on the cityscape of Rouen on May 30, 1431? I am visiting the spectacular "Rouen 1431" 360° Panorama, by the artist Yadegar Asisi, housed in a purpose-built tower on the right

Figure 1. Rouen 1431 panorama.
Photo by Thomas Boivin © Asisi.

bank of the River Seine in the modern city. Developed from sketches and drawings of the medieval city, as well as historical models and documentary evidence, the Panorama is built from a composite of photography (including costumed re-enactors) and computer-generated imagery, offering a hyper-real, immersive view of the late-medieval landscape. Viewed from a fifteen-metre-high platform, changing lighting creates a cycle from day to night, and sound-effects evoke the aural landscape of the medieval city.

The Panorama offers a fantasy, an impossible view of Gothic Rouen, experienced by 170,000 visitors in its opening year. It also plays a major role in current regeneration of this area of the city's right bank—away from the established heritage tourism attractions, in a zone characterized by post-industrial warehouses and hangars—and regional development: the city's medieval past at the forefront of local political agendas to "boldly combine heritage and modernity."[3] But the Panorama offers something other than a straightforward reconstruction of the medieval city: it presents a view which was always impossible—one which never existed. I stand looking down on Rouen, 1431, from the top of the cathedral's Butter Tower—not built until the sixteenth century. In the streets below me, moments from across the city's year are conflated into a single day. I can see the Saint Roman Privilege and Ascension Day procession in the Place de le Calende, and Mystery Play performers in the streets, while, at the corner of the derelict Saint Herbland Church, I glimpse a wooden cart carrying a young woman—Joan of Arc—to the stake.

In the book which accompanies "Rouen 1431," Asisi reflects on the ways in which his installation participates in the tradition of the panorama, which emerged as a popular form of artwork and visitor experience in later eighteenth- and early nineteenth-century Europe. These historical panoramas—often depicting city views—were continuous 360°-representations, hung in specially-constructed rotundas similar to the present-day version built by Asisi. The huge dimensions of these works, together with their manipulation of perspective, produced the illusion of being transported to a new place, presenting paying visitors with landscape—and especially cityscape—as a carefully-managed and highly-crafted spectacle (see Further Reading at the end of this book). Before the technology of panoramas, this pleasure of commanding the full view of a landscape was expressed in the early modern tradition of "long views" and "prospect views," such as the hugely popular depictions of English towns and cities published by Samuel and Nathaniel Buck in the 1730s and 40s.

Across their various technologies, the formal tropes of these prospect and panorama views served to reinforce the "cityscape" as an aesthetic ideal, achieved through an idealized—often fantasized—perspective, and called into a coherent, unified, pleasing whole. The term "cityscape" is a relative latecomer to the vocabulary of place and space, first appearing in print as a playful correlate to (rural) "landscape" in 1856 (Oxford English Dictionary). But, as this first citation illustrates, its formation plays upon the currency of "landscape" in English usage from at least 1605. A borrow-

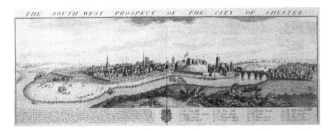

Figure 2. Nathaniel Buck, SW prospect of the
City of Chester, 1728 (British Library Maps K.Top.9.7.b),
by permission of the British Library

ing from the Dutch *landschap*—a technical term for natural
scenery in a painting—"landscape" is thus fundamentally
an aesthetic construct, framed by cultural conventions, values, and desires. These carry over into its urban analogue:
the "cityscape," every bit as much, is a product of aesthetic
tropes and received representational practices or ways of
seeing. Representation of a cityscape always involves some
sleight of hand or elision; its perception demands some willing complicity on the part of the viewer. The idea of "cityscape" forges an aesthetic whole out of the disparate, fragmentary, accidental elements of the built urban environment,
replacing rupture, dissonance, and contradiction with unity
and coherence. It obstructs our attention to the collisions,
frictions, and incongruities in the material environment, as
well as to the contested and fractured nature of the city as
a fraught nexus of multiple practised social spaces. But the
"cityscape" endures as a compelling trope; one, for example,
that continues to motivate and frame the tourist gaze and
inform the marketing of urban heritage today. It's in the title
of this book, too, and while I use it throughout my discussion
as a near synonym for "urban environment" or "geographical
space of the city," it carries with it cultural and aesthetic con-
notations to which I will return in the closing "Afterword." For
now, surveying the spectacular cityscape of Rouen, 1431, in

Asisi's Panorama, I know that I need to take myself down into the streets below.

I walk into Rouen city centre with my family and explore. We stroll around the cathedral—looking upwards from ground level, this time—and take photographs of the Gros Horloge astronomical clock. We browse shops in the medieval streets, and buy a postcard of a Monet painting of the Notre Dame towers. My five-year-old daughter plays Pokemon Go, encountering the city through the screen of a phone. We sit outside a café and eat crêpes, while soldiers carrying automatic weapons walk by amongst the tourists: this is summer 2016 and a priest has been murdered by terrorists in a nearby church. I think of Rouen in 1431 or 1090, with soldiers on the streets and tension in the air. This is the medieval cityscape today: a series of appositions, frictions, and dialogues which bring the historic city into focus in shifting and sometimes surprising ways within the modern urban environment. As Sarah Salih has recently noted, seeing the medieval city around us is not a calculated and predictable process of empirical recovery. Instead, it often requires "effort, imagination, luck, or knowledge," contingent on the moment and on individual perspective, not fixed or replicable.[4]

My experiences in Rouen highlight the complexities and challenges inherent in understanding what constitutes the medieval cityscape today. Perhaps most obviously, the medieval cityscape comprises the historic built environment and the material heritage of the Middle Ages in surviving buildings and architectural fragments, as well as in features of street pattern and urban layout. David Lowenthal has commented on the "supreme merit of tangible remains," inherent in "the ready access they afford to the past's ubiquitous traces," adding that:

> Relics and remnants viewable by all offer unmediated impressions free to any passer-by. Seeing history on the ground is less self-conscious than reading about it: texts require both an author and out deliberate engagement, whereas relics can come to us seemingly unguided and without conscious effort.[5]

Yet Lowenthal's optimism about ubiquity and accessibility jars with Salih's observations on the often elusive, fugitive nature of the medieval cityscape—sometimes evading view, sometimes slipping into focus. And even here, in the case of the city's tangible heritage, the medieval is mediated through ongoing processes of conservation, reconstruction, imitation, and adaptation. As always, we view the Middle Ages through the accretions, interventions, and responses of later centuries, as the material medieval cityscape continues to evolve and change. Alongside the tangible survivals of stones and timber, intangible heritage also plays an important role in shaping place and identity. In relation to the medieval cityscape, we might consider the significance of traditional practices which survive from the Middle Ages, local stories, memories, the mythologies encoded in street names, civic festivals, and religious rituals. The interplay between tangible and intangible heritage in historic environments is now well recognized and understood by scholars, heritage practitioners, and conservation bodies.

But, today, the medieval cityscape must also be understood in new terms, with radical implications for how we think about place, heritage, and modes of encounter with the past and with historic environments. Increasingly, the medieval cityscape is becoming virtual or digital: not constrained or limited by the vagaries of material survival or embodied performance in the physical environment. As our cities become more complex, hybrid spaces, in which material and digital worlds overlay and intersect, so the medieval cityscape is being re-conceptualized as a space composed of both physical and virtual content. Digital technologies and media are producing new kinds of augmented or hybrid medieval cityscape, using tools such as 3D visualizations, interactive applications, map overlays, gaming, and geo-location data to forge connections between present-day urban environments and their antecedents, and to situate individuals in immersive and engaging historic landscapes. These technological changes are fundamentally transforming the ways in which we approach questions of research, conservation, and interpretation, offering new methodologies for recuperating lost heritage, for mediating between empirical, evidence-based scholarship and more speculative versions of the past, and for enabling richer varieties of visitor experience. In the context of these emergent, rapidly-developing digital technologies, we can understand the augmented or hybrid medieval cityscape today as an incipient space: just drawing into focus as a new realm of experience and critical inquiry.

The space of possibility opened up by these developing technologies is also mirrored in current scholarly approaches to the medieval city. Where, for example, the "Rouen 1431" Panorama uses computer-generated imagery alongside photography of surviving monuments to produce its composite version of the medieval city, it also deliberately exceeds the limitations of partial historical evidence—and even the restrictions of factual history—to present suggestive juxtapositions, catalyze affective engagement, and provoke critical questions. Similarly, in much current research on the medieval city, we can see an increasingly self-conscious imbrication of empirical scholarship and creative re-imagining, and experimentation with a wider variety of tools and idioms for academic engagement with the past. Such approaches expand the roles of researchers, allowing room for creative practice alongside empirical analysis. They resonate with current debates, often led by medievalist scholars, which seek to interrogate, challenge, and renew modes of scholarship in the Humanities, and to explore alternative critical registers and sites of inquiry. Like viewing fifteenth-century Rouen from the top of a tower which didn't yet exist, these experimental modes play with new vantage-points and different ways of seeing, opening up new perspectives on the medieval cityscape and fresh critical conversations.

This book will draw on my own background working with medieval cityscapes today, bringing together research with heritage interpretation practice and participation in urban conservation and regeneration initiatives. In particular, the book is grounded on two major projects—both inter-disciplinary and collaborative—which I have led over the past decade, in the UK cities of Chester (north-west England) and Swansea (south Wales). "Mapping Medieval Chester: Place and Identity in an English Borderland City, c.1200–1500" (www.medievalchester.ac.uk) explored a variety of textual and cartographic "mappings" of this medieval city, to explore how the urban space was understood and represented differently by individuals and communities from different cultural and ethnic backgrounds. The project produced a new interactive digital atlas of Chester, ca. 1500, using Geographical Information Systems (GIS) technology, linked to textual "mappings" of the city in Latin (*De Laude Cestrie* by the monk Lucian, ca. 1200, as well as the poem to Chester in Higden's *Polychronicon*), English (Henry Bradshaw's *Life of St. Werburge*, printed in 1521), and Welsh (various poems from manuscript sources, including satire and invective directed against the city as a site of colonialist control, as well as devotional poetry addressed to the relics of the cross at St. John's Church). This research then formed the basis for a long-term partnership with Cheshire West and Chester Council (local government), and especially the city's Grosvenor Museum. Collaborative activities, shaped by the new research into the medieval city, included development of a permanent public art installation at St. John's Church (and regeneration of the area around the site), a major museum exhibition and public activities, an interactive city tour website, and consultation on issues from public realm policy and wayfinding strategy to conservation, planning, and heritage interpretation (http://discover.medievalchester.ac.uk). The second core project which underpins this book is focused on Swansea, a post-industrial port city on the south Wales coast; in the Middle Ages the administrative centre of the Anglo-Norman colonial marcher lordship of Gower. "City Witness: Place and Perspective in Medieval Swansea" (www.medievalswansea.ac.uk) took as its starting point a story which has attracted attention from several medieval historians: the accounts of the hanging of the Welsh outlaw William Cragh in 1290 (and his apparently miraculous revival) contained in the canonization proceedings for Thomas Cantilupe, Bishop of Hereford, preserved in a manuscript in the Vatican Library (shelfmark MS Vat. Lat. 4015). The project produced digital editions and translations of the nine medieval eyewitness statements reporting the events surrounding Cragh's execution, linked to an interactive digital atlas of Swansea ca. 1300 with itinerary maps and 3D sight-line visualizations for each witness. Again, the research in Swansea was intrinsically connected to local urban regeneration and development agendas. In fact, the research was initiated in response to a request from the City and County of Swansea (local government) for support with interpreting Swansea Castle—the only surviving material element of the medieval cityscape—and developing a distinctive identity for the city centre (an economically deprived area targeted for regeneration) as a heritage site. The project involved advising and consulting with the Council and commercial companies, a museum exhibition and public events, and production of a trail around Swansea city centre, with markers set into pedestrian pavement walkways. The project continues to expand and develop, with the creation of a new heritage tourism route (The St. Thomas Way) from Swansea to Hereford Cathedral, inspired by the pilgrimage made by the hanged man, Cragh—together with his would-be executioners—after his miraculous revival.

These projects bridge conventional scholarship and heritage practice, modelling the ways in which research into the historic urban environment can impact on medieval cityscapes today. They also demonstrate the productive kinds of exchange and reciprocal benefit which can emerge from working with practitioners and professionals outside academia, and from working in creative modes, or in contexts driven by specific real-world agendas and pressures. The projects also both deal with the medieval cityscape in its various inter-related forms: from analysis of medieval evidence in order to recover historic places and spatial practices, to engagement with and intervention in the material environment today, to experimentation with virtual (digital) versions of the medieval city in order to test research hypotheses and engage the wider public. Indeed, the "Discover Medieval Chester" website, with an interactive layered map of the medieval and modern city, and multi-media tour resources, received a commendation award (New Year Honours, 2014) from the Chester Civic Trust, a body dedicated to safeguarding the heritage of the city's built environment. This was the first time that a digital initiative (rather than conservation of a physical building, or new building developments within the city) had been recognized by the Trust—a significant marker of the ways in which the medieval cityscape increasingly encompasses both the material and virtual realms.

So, my own work on medieval cityscapes crosses from traditional scholarship on the Middle Ages into heritage interpretation and management, and connects research with applied practice. But my own disciplinary background is in medieval cultural history and, specifically, medieval literary studies. What's distinctive about a book on "Medieval Cityscapes Today" written by an author with a training in literary history and textual studies rather than, for example, a specialist in historical geography, or an archaeologist, or a heritage scientist? While my work, and this book's discussions, touch on all of these areas, I cannot claim primary expertise in these disciplines. Instead, my approach to the medieval cityscape is informed by the techniques of close reading and analysis I learned as the core skills of my scholarly specialism, and the attention to story-telling, representation, and reception which I seek to bring to any kind of cultural product. I am interested in the city as a locus of multi-layered stories, and as a site where meanings and identities are constantly produced and negotiated. My interest in the medieval cityscape begins as much with reading as with material culture: from the Vatican manuscript recording William Cragh's execution, with its strange textual geographies and half-remembered itineraries, to a Middle English poem which (somewhat preposterously) compares a fire in Chester to the sack of Troy or the fall of Rome. These imagined versions of the medieval city are every bit as significant as its physical realities in the Middle Ages, or its present-day material and virtual landscapes. For some readers, my approach may suggest the influence of literary "Psychogeography" and the work of writers such as Will Self, Iain Sinclair, or Peter Ackroyd (see Further Reading). While this is not an approach I have consciously attempted to adopt, I find their model of place as a way into stories both public and personal (and sometimes autobiographical) attractive and compelling. Lastly, I am also interested in how post-medieval sources, from the early modern period onwards, negotiate questions of how to engage with, conserve or recuperate, and make sense of medieval history and its material survivals in the urban landscape. Thus, I situate our current concerns about the constitution, conservation, and curation of medieval cityscapes within a longer-view context of critical and practical discourses on the subject.

This book is structured into two sections, focusing on the complementary and contrasting case-study cities of Chester and Swansea, and drawing on my research and heritage management work in these locations. Each section is built around a series of itineraries through the cityscape, from a stroll through Chester to St. John's Church (following in the footsteps of Henry James and the medieval monk Lucian), to the medieval witness routes and the modern pavement marker trail—as well as a walk down the High Street taken by Dylan Thomas, the famous local poet—in Swansea. The paired case studies of Chester and Swansea allow interrogation of some shared themes and questions across the two locations, including their particular characteristics as borderland cities and sites of complex multi-lingual, multi-ethnic cultures in the Middle Ages. But, more emphatically, the two cities offer a striking contrast which allows investigation of medieval cityscapes today in radically different forms. Chester is well established as a tourist destination (though more usually marketed for its Roman, rather than medieval, heritage), and boasts impressive material survivals from the Middle Ages, including its churches and cathedral, the intact circuit of its city walls, and vernacular architecture (though, as we shall see, many of these buildings have been subject to heavy restoration and later adaptation). For well over a century, visitors have travelled from across the world to experience the city's picturesque medieval cityscape and, more recently, to share in modern revivals of its intangible medieval heritage, such as the five-yearly staging of the Chester Mystery Play cycle or the annual Minstrels' Court festival of musicians. The medieval cityscape of Swansea, by contrast, is almost invisible today, due to wartime bombing and later urban re-development. Swansea Castle survives as the only immediately-recognizable fragment of medieval material heritage in the urban environment, now cast adrift in a post-war street layout and a city centre scoured of most of its historic architecture and tangible relationship to the past. While the nearby Gower Peninsula—a government-designated "Area of Outstanding Natural Beauty"—preserves a still-visible medieval landscape in its churches, villages (including traces of lost settlements), and field patterns, the urban environment of Swansea suppresses and denies its rich medieval past. In their contrasting cityscapes, Chester and Swansea present emphatically different challenges and opportunities for academic research into the medieval urban environment, and for heritage management and interpretation practice.

One city offers a rich, tangible medieval cityscape which demands careful conservation and curation for visitors and local communities. The other raises questions about how we—whether as scholars or heritage practitioners—might begin to engage with an absent historic cityscape and the challenges of mediating between the modern city and its lost antecedents. The case study of medieval Swansea—like the Rouen Panorama, among the post-industrial warehouses on the River Seine—also opens up questions about the relationships between heritage interpretation or exploitation, economic and social need, and urban regeneration and development. In what ways can scholars of the medieval past participate in the management and renewal of cities—including those facing crises of economics or identity—today?

In the spirit of this "Past Imperfect" series, this book attempts to break down divides between the medieval and modern, between disciplinary boundaries, and between typical notions of the distinction between "research" and "creative practice." It seeks to offer provocations and challenges to conventional conceptualizations of scholarship and its limits. Its discussion of imbricated research and applied practice in relation to medieval cityscapes today has wider-reaching implications as a manifesto for thinking in new ways about the public value of Humanities research, and the ways in which a range of scholarly disciplines might claim a stake in the production of the public realm in our towns and cities. But the book also acknowledges the challenges, compromises, and risks involved when traditional, established methods of scholarly research are enlarged to accommodate new kinds of creative, collaborative, and public-facing practice.

The title of Chapter 1, "The Medieval City and Other Monsters," recalls Michael Camille's description of medieval sites as "continually being reinterpreted, reconstructed, and interrupted by new monsters of our own making,"[6] but takes it cue most immediately from the epigraph to an eighteenth-century Chester text. This chapter, focused on Chester, begins by inviting the reader to join me for a walk through Chester's streets from the medieval Cathedral of St. Werburgh to the Collegiate Church of St. John, re-tracing and intersecting with fragments of other itineraries and accounts of the city reaching back to the Middle Ages. Via its route through the cityscape of Chester, the chapter explores the history of the management and representation of the city's medieval built heritage, raising questions about perception, conservation, and idioms of scholarly and popular reception. The chapter then focuses on the public art project at the city's medieval St. John's ruins, on which I collaborated as part of the "Discover Medieval Chester" project, funded by the UK Arts and Humanities Research Council. I approach the art project in the context of a long tradition of discussions of heritage conservation in Chester, drawing particularly on an eighteenth-century pamphlet, which, through its Ovidian epigraph, raises the perennial challenge of "restoring ancient forms" without creating "new monsters." The chapter opens out into a broader discussion of questions of authority, legitimacy, and licence in historical scholarship, and the ways in which practice-led or creative research problematizes conventional disciplines and categories. The chapter concludes with a vision of engaged research which defies the threat of "monsters" and which embraces new forms of playful, experimental exchange and collaboration, opening up richer possibilities for academics to engage and intervene in historic cityscapes today.

Chapter 2 focuses on the city of Swansea, beginning with Dylan Thomas as he walks through the "havoc'd" centre of the bombed-out town on a freezing February day, encountering the ghosts of "vanished buildings" in a post-war landscape of "snow and ruin." Titled "Seeing the Invisible City: Spatial Encounters in Medieval Swansea," the chapter asks questions about how we might begin to recover and interpret lost or absent medieval cityscapes, and models possible approaches through the digital and material strategies which formed elements of the "City Witness" research project. The chapter examines the nine witness depositions collected in the early thirteenth-century MS Vat. Lat. 4015, informed by GIS mapping and reconstruction of the witnesses' itineraries and movements within medieval Swansea. This analysis offers new insights into the physical landscape of the medieval town, but also calls attention to the always-invisible social and cultural geographies which operated within the urban environment, and which shaped and constrained the spatial practices of individuals from different cultural and ethnic communities. The chapter explores the production of a pavement (sidewalk) marker trail, linked to digital resources and virtual reconstructions of the medieval town, as a way of engaging modern communities and visitors with the city's unseen medieval history. It raises questions about conventional paradigms in heritage interpretation practice, which rely on physical "relics" or material continuities between past and present as a conduit into history, suggesting instead that experiences of rupture, dislocation, and disorientation can provide an equally powerful impetus to imaginative engagement with the past. Through its discussion of medieval sources and modern responses, the chapter presents and interrogates a series of inter-linked, multi-layered invisible cityscapes: from the complex cultural and social geographies of the town in the Middle Ages, to the landscapes of memory and recollection conjured by Dylan Thomas and the medieval witnesses, to the absent medieval cityscape of Swansea today, juxtaposed with the virtual visualizations of the medieval town on the digital tour website. The chapter also explores other invisible geographies which haunt the modern city, from the grand re-development proposals for Swansea after the Blitz—which were never realized—to counter-factual descriptions of the city which imagine the results of different approaches to conservation and urban planning in the post-war period. In the cityscape today, past and present, real and imagined, fact and fiction collide, pull against each other and overlay in surprising, uncomfortable and endlessly suggestive ways.

A short Afterword once again begins with autobiography, and a day filming for a television documentary in Winchester (summer 2017). It returns critically to the vexed ideal of "cityscape," and the challenges of presenting a fragmentary, multi-layered historic environment in a coherent and engaging way via broadcast media. Bringing together primary evidence, individual experience, story-telling, and current theories of place and temporality, this section foregrounds the fundamental roles of time and desire in our engagements with the historic urban environment.

Notes

[1] *The Ecclesiastical History of Orderic Vitalis IV*, ed. and trans. Marjorie Chibnall (Oxford: Clarendon Press, 1969), 224; this translation from Leonie V. Hicks, "Through the City Streets: Movement and Space in Rouen as Seen by the Norman Chroniclers," in *Society and Culture in Medieval Rouen, 911–1300*, ed. Leonie Hicks and Elma Brenner (Turnhout: Brepols, 2013), 125–49 at 136–37.

[2] Michel de Certeau, *The Practice of Everyday Life*, trans. Steven Rendall (Berkeley: University of California Press, 1988), 92–93.

[3] Frédéric Sanchex, President of Métropole Rouen Normandie, in *Rouen 1431: Yadegar Asisi 360° Panorama* (Berlin: Asisi Editions, 2016), 5.

[4] Sarah Salih, 'In/visible Medieval/isms', *Studies in Medievalism* 25 (2016): 53–69 at 53.

[5] David Lowenthal, *The Past is a Foreign Country Revisited* (Cambridge: Cambridge University Press, 2015), 393.

[6] Camille is referring here specifically to medieval cathedrals. Michael Camille, *The Gargoyles of Notre-Dame: Medievalism and the Monsters of Modernity* (Chicago: University of Chicago Press, 2009), xi.

Chapter 1

Chester: The Medieval City and Other Monsters

This chapter sets out on a walk through Chester's streets, before going on to explore the historical management and representation of the city's medieval built heritage, and then moving into a broader discussion of questions of authority, legitimacy, and licence in historical scholarship, and how we might conduct engaged research which defies the threat of various "monsters."

Walking through Chester's History

We begin our walk outside the south porch of Chester's great medieval cathedral, today dedicated to Christ and the Blessed Virgin Mary, but, in the Middle Ages, the Benedictine abbey of the city's patron saint, St. Werburgh. Beneath the red sandstone walls of the south aisle and south transept, we move through the cathedral grounds, past the city war memorial, completed in 1922 in a Gothic style which echoes its medieval surroundings, and out through a wrought-iron gate onto the pavement. Following the curve of St. Werburgh's Street, with its ornate half-timbered buildings and smart boutiques, we turn onto Eastgate Street, where a view of Chester's famous "Rows" stretches out before us. Here we jostle with crowds of shoppers, street entertainers, and buskers, and, perhaps, horserace-goers stepping out of the glossy Grosvenor Hotel in sharp suits and flamboyant hats. Today, as always, we'll also step aside for tour groups and visitors clutching brochures and cameras, as they follow their guide's uplifted umbrella or study their tourist maps, and take in the prospect of Chester's rich and evocative built heritage.

Perhaps the most iconic feature of the city's surviving medieval fabric, the Rows of Chester run along the four main streets, where the terraced, mostly half-timbered buildings incorporate galleried public walkways at first-floor level, running largely continuously along the length of the streets. Today, these galleries give access to shop fronts at this upper level, while the undercroft space below would originally have been used for storage and later, certainly by the sixteenth century, as workshops, taverns, and further shops. Writing in 1584, William Smith comments on the convenience and uniqueness of the Rows, observing that:

> The Buildings of the City are very ancient; and the Houses builded in such sort, that a man may go dry, from one place of the City to another, and never come in the street; but go as it were in Gallaries, which they call, The Roes, which have Shops on both sides, and underneath, with divers fair staires to go up or down into the street. Which manner of building, I have not heard of in any place of Christendome.[7]

These distinctive galleried buildings probably developed in the thirteenth century—a period of prosperity and importance for Chester as the base for Edward I's campaigns in Wales—entering the textual record in 1293 and referred to unambiguously as "Rows" by 1356.[8] The medieval Rows encompassed buildings of varying size and prestige, though all would have been the dwellings of "the relatively prosperous trading and merchant classes."[9] While the exact origins and influences of the Rows remain a subject of debate, the survival of much of their medieval material fabric has been described as "special" and "probably unmatched in any other English city centre."[10] It is this material link to Chester's medieval history—and the picturesque appearance of these unusual buildings—which appeals to the city's many visitors. The Rows feature on postcards, souvenir magnets, mugs, and boxes of fudge. They offer indispensable cover for tour groups on rainy days, and an immersive sense of walking within the city's history, looking down on its streets from a vantage-point framed by the past.

Yet, as we pause and look up at the Rows today, alongside other visitors to Chester, the view before us tells a much more complicated story, of unknowns, lacunae, transformation, and re-invention. These iconic, celebrated survivals obscure the "important and startling gaps" which remain in our understanding of their place in medieval Chester (Ward, p. 48): not only their early development, but also the kinds of structures they replaced, and the buildings and lives more typical of the city's less wealthy, ordinary inhabitants. More arrestingly, the fabric we see at street level and above retains little authentic medieval detail. The Rows were substantially altered and adapted in the early modern period, as social and commercial needs changed, including the installation of stallboards (so that the galleried walkways could be flanked with shops on either side), enclosure of sections of gallery into private property, and extension of upper levels on posts over the street. By the nineteenth century, the Rows had begun to appeal to the city's increasing numbers of tourists, and were also recognised as significant historic survivals by groups such as the Chester Archaeological Society. Conservation and reconstruction work on the Rows changed their character radically, from the profusion of half-timbered vernacular revival buildings produced by local architects John Douglas and T. M. Lockwood, to the construction of the classically-styled Chester Bank at the east end of Eastgate Street North in 1860, and the high Victorian Gothic of Brown's department store on Eastgate Street South. While Brown's retains its medieval undercroft with vaulted ceiling—now the department store café—the architecture at street level is grander, more ornate, and certainly at a larger scale than the original Rows structures, and has little to do with medieval building techniques or idioms. Yet the black and white, half-timbered style of the Victorian buildings on Eastgate Street and, behind us, on St. Werburgh's Street, deliberately evokes an imagined picturesque past, fulfilling our expectations of a charming, historic

England even as it invents and shapes them. A largely nineteenth-century confection, the Rows on Eastgate Street offer us a version of the medieval cityscape which rejects literal conservation in favour of more immediately recognizable, legible, and appealing aesthetic markers of premodernity.

From the Rows, we turn and walk towards Chester's Eastgate, set in the city's historic walls. The circuit of walls dates back to Roman times, though most of the surviving fabric visible today is medieval, and here at the Eastgate it was replaced in the late eighteenth century by an elliptical brick arch with a walkway above and pedestrian arches below on either side. The ornate ironwork clock above the arch—a late nineteenth-century addition—is reputedly the second most-photographed clock in Britain, after that of the Elizabeth Tower (commonly known as Big Ben) in London.[11] In the Middle Ages, goods and livestock were brought into the city here, with tariffs charged for commodities such as wool, salt, coal, turf, and timber, as well as items such as knives, cups, dishes, and tankards. These charges applied to merchandise brought into the city from beyond Cheshire, while goods from within the city were exempt. The Eastgate was one of the city's four main gates, where such tolls could be paid in cash.[12]

From its earliest appearances in the literary record, however, the Eastgate has a symbolic significance equal to its important economic role. In his late twelfth-century encomium to Chester, *De Laude Cestrie*, the monk Lucian re-imagines his home city—on the western border of England and almost the edge of the known world—as a powerful centre which looks out onto the whole globe. Lucian plays creatively with the views from the city's four gates: striking raised vantage-points in their position set in the defensive walls and elevated above most other buildings. From the west, Lucian writes, Chester looks out over Ireland, from the Northgate over Norway and the far north, and from the southern gate over Wales. From the Eastgate, the text announces, Chester "prospectat Indiam" ("looks towards India"), towards the distant and exotic, towards trade and wealth: the assertive gaze of an ambitious and prosperous city of the world.[13] The

Eastgate gathers a range of symbolic names and meanings in *De Laude Cestrie*, reflecting Lucian's propensity to read the city exegetically, as an allegorical text which reveals truths of divine order and providential history. Located in the direction of St. John's Church, at the south-eastern edge of Chester, the Eastgate becomes for Lucian "John's Gate," protected by John the Baptist, forming a symbolic "specula" ("watch tower") over the world (fol. 22v, marginal note). It is also the "porta solis" ("sun's gate"), aligned with the rising dawn and, allegorically, with John as the forerunner and harbinger of the spiritual light of Christ's incarnation (fol. 24v). These symbolic medieval cityscapes are no longer obvious to viewers of the Eastgate today (and indeed it is unclear how far these specific tropes were ever current beyond Lucian's somewhat idiosyncratic work). Yet the visitors admiring the Eastgate and its clock today recognize, in varying ways, that this is a significant site, its material fabric and meanings shaped and re-shaped by ongoing intervention and representation—just as their own photographs affirm and reproduce its scenic value now.

We pass through the Eastgate now, and walk down St. John's Street. At the southern end, on Little St. John's Street, we find the remains of Chester's Amphitheatre, a survival from its pre-medieval history and its foundation as the Roman fortress of Deva. Today, as so often, a group of schoolchildren is gathered in the central arena, while a guide dressed as a Roman centurion explains the story of the place. The Roman history of Chester has been celebrated for centuries and historically privileged over the city's medieval heritage, with significant consequences for its heritage tourism offering today. John Speed's map of Chester, published in *The Theatre of the Empire of Great Britain* (1611), is a striking example of this trend, valorizing Chester's Roman origins through a series of visual signifiers, and, through its popularity and wide transmission, helping to shape perceptions of the city and its history from the early modern period onwards.[14] Speed's aerial view of Chester makes clearly visible the grid layout inherited from the city's Roman foundation, with four medallions at the right-hand of the image commemorating the Roman emperors Julius Caesar (who began the process of conquering Britain in the first century BC), Vespasian and Domitian, as well as the "Legio XX Victrix," the "Twentieth Victorious Legion" which participated in the Roman invasion of Britain in AD 43 and was subsequently stationed at the fortress of Deva Vitrix (Chester). In Daniel King's *The Vale-Royall of England* (1656), William Smith gathers the available evidence for Chester's Roman origins and concludes that "if we should date the *Epocha* of *Chesters* nativity at the vulgar year of Christ, 61, it wants at this time but five years of being a 1000. years old, which I think is a gallant age, especially seeing she breaks but little, and holds her Complexion so bravely." He goes on to note that the "Romans residence in great numbers and plenty, their arched Vaults, and sweating houses, their Urns, Coins, tessellated Pavements, do abundantly witnesse" (p. 6).

The venerable age and prestigious classical associations of Roman Chester played a major part in the formation and promotion of the city's identity in the post-medieval period. But Roman Chester was visible in the Middle Ages, too, and for many medieval inhabitants of the city, the sense of living in an ancient cityscape seems to have been acutely present. Ranulph Higden's poem on Chester, in his *Polychronicon*, names the city as "Legecastria [...] vel Urbs Legionum" ("Legecastria [...] or the City of Legions"), imagining the city's landscape through classical mythology. The great city walls, he suggests playfully, are "velut Hercules actus" ("like a deed of Hercules") and "Mars et Mercurius, Bacchus, Venus, atque Laverna, / Proteus et Pluto regna tenent inibi" ("Mars and Mercury, Bacchus, Venus and Laverna, / Proteus and Pluto reign in that place").[15] Clearly, many medieval Cestrians understood themselves to be inhabiting a landscape of antiquity, an urban environment littered with the suggestive traces of remote, mythic history.

However, the prestige and appeal of Chester's Roman origins have presented problematic implications for the management and interpretation of its medieval heritage in recent centuries. Chester archaeologist Simon Ward observes that "[r]eviews of the archaeological evidence for medieval Chester are notable for their scarcity and their negative slant," contrasting this with the emphasis on investigation of the Roman city. Indeed, he notes that "the bulk of the early [archaeological] records concern only the Roman period" (p. 31), and that Chester gained a reputation "for being interested only in the Roman period and nothing else" (p. 33). This imbalance in part reflects a perceived hierarchy of cultural value, inherited from the earliest Renaissance and early modern antiquarian traditions. But, as Ward acknowledges, practical considerations also play a role, with medieval archaeological evidence in Chester less plentiful and often more difficult to recover than Roman material. Here at Chester Amphitheatre, the competing cultural narratives provided by different imagined histories come sharply into focus. While the surviving material fabric is a legacy of the city's Roman past, more recent hypotheses have linked the site to a mythic, quasi-medieval insular history. A flurry of media coverage in 2010 followed a proposition that Chester Amphitheatre was in fact King Arthur's Camelot, with a stone altar at the centre forming the famous Round Table. The *Daily Telegraph* announced that "Historians Locate King Arthur's Round Table" (July 11, 2010), while the History Channel screened the documentary film "King Arthur's Round Table Revealed" (July 19, 2010). Once again, varying popular perceptions of distant pasts and fantasies of the medieval become overlaid and entangled in the material cityscape of Chester and its imaginative interpretation.

A few steps on from the Amphitheatre, we reach the final destination of our walking tour: the Collegiate Church of St. John. An imposing edifice of Romanesque and early Gothic red sandstone (though significantly changed since the Middle Ages), the church also retains the ruins of its fourteenth-century chancel, Lady Chapel and choir (destroyed in the Reformation) at its eastern end. Once the cathedral of Chester, the church had a chequered history in the Middle Ages, especially when it lost its place as the principal church of the Diocese of

Lichfield (by 1102) and, later, when the abbey of St. Werburgh became the new cathedral for the city after the Dissolution. The church has Anglo-Saxon origins, with some early commentators even ascribing its foundation to King Æthelræd of Mercia in the late seventh or early eighth century.[16] In an early sixteenth-century text, Henry Bradshaw, a monk at the abbey of St. Werburgh, presents St. John's as a key location in a seminal moment of Anglo-Saxon history: the visit of King Edgar to Chester in 973, where he is rowed along the River Dee by eight tributary kings in an act of submission and allegiance. While stories of this event owe much to later tradition and little to original pre-Conquest evidence, Bradshaw, like other medieval historiographers, regards the episode as emblematic of emergent English nationhood. He describes the pageantry of Edgar's ceremonial passage up the Dee, and the crucial moment in his performance of royal power which takes place here, notably outside the city walls, after he has slipped through a "priue posturne," then "[r]owing vpward to the churche of saynt Iohn."[17] The ritual at St. John's incorporates a public act of devotion to the cross, as well as the only direct speech from Edgar himself which is included in Bradshaw's account.

> Whan the kynge had done his pylgrimage
> And to the holy roode [cross] made oblacion,
> They entred agayne into the sayd barge,
> Passynge to his place with great renowne.
> Than Edgare spake in praysnge of the crowne:
> "All my successours may glad and ioyfull be
> To haue suche homage, honour and dignite."
>
> (lines 1185–91)

While later medieval accounts such as that of Bradshaw rely on popular traditions and the authority of post-Conquest chroniclers, there is early documentary and archaeological evidence for the importance of St. John's in the Anglo-Saxon period. Textual and material survivals from St. John's, then, take us on a tantalising imaginative journey back to the early medieval Chester of Saxons and Vikings, Æthelflæd, Lady of the Mercians, and her reputed reconstruction of the city's Roman walls, and even St. Werburgh herself, the Mercian noblewoman adopted as the city's patron saint.

Our path from Chester Cathedral, formerly the abbey of St. Werburgh, to the church of St. John evokes and intersects with fragments of other itineraries reaching back to the Middle Ages. Our approach to St. John's overlays the journeys of medieval Welsh pilgrims, who made their way here to venerate the relics of the True Cross held in the church in the later Middle Ages. A substantial body of medieval Welsh poetry celebrates the arrival of fragments of the cross in Chester, washed in on the "llanw" ("tide"), and their healing powers for those who pray to them.[18] In the fifteenth century, Chester's civic Corpus Christi processions, led by guilds and part of the pageant tradition which led to the flowering of its Mystery Play cycle, culminated at St. John's Church.[19] The last stretch of our route, approaching St. John's, also reflects another, more personal, medieval journey, described in Lucian's *De Laude Cestrie*. Lucian reports the events of one particular day, in which:

Nam pro responso monasterii missus et curiam comitis aditurus, post missas in basilica Archangeli Michaelis explicitas, temporalis negocii certitudinem nactus, eciam uenerandi precursoris ecclesiam credidi uisitandam, quo potens meritis, exaudicione piissimus, Eterni Regis clementiam uotis omnium impetraret.

Having been sent with the monastery's answer and about to visit the earl's residence, after hearing masses in the church of the Archangel Michael, and having obtained confidence to conduct my earthly business, I thought it also worth visiting the church of our venerable predecessor, where that virtuous and most piously devoted man can obtain the mercy of the eternal king for everyone who requests it. (fol. 5r)

Lucian's highly allegorical, homiletic style transforms a quotidian walk in the city into a symbolic, instructive event: having left the abbey of St. Werburgh and attended masses at the church of St. Michael, he takes a diversion to St. John's ("the church of our venerable predecessor") before completing his business at the castle ("the earl's residence"). Typically for Lucian, the built environment of Chester is inhabited with spiritual meanings and didactic potential. He shares with his reader his sense of a contrast between the secular and ecclesiastical spaces of the city, and the particular spiritual solace and calm he finds at St. John's: "castellum tedio, set ecclesia solatio fuit" ("the castle was a nuisance, but the church was a consolation," fol. 5r).

Our path to St. John's also traces many of the routes integral to the early development of antiquarian and visitor interest in Chester's historic cityscape. Already in Daniel King's *Vale-Royall of England*, published in 1656, the idea of exploring the city's heritage through a scenic walk is well established enough for William Webb to use it as the central conceit in his topographical description of the city. Webb introduces his account of Chester with the metaphor of walking ("I have chosen this way to walk in," p. 2), and then explicitly leads the reader on a tour of the walls and streets of the city. He begins his "circuit of the Wall" at the Eastgate, later adding "As I led you even now about the walls of the city, which was no very long walk; so I now desire you would be acquainted with the streets and lanes" (p. 20), inviting the reader "to step from thence into THE CITY itself" and guiding them in a journey through the city's built heritage, measured in "paces" and presented as an intimate stroll through place and history. Indeed, by the early nineteenth century, a proliferation of guide books and pamphlets were available for visitors to Chester, offering them routes by which the city's historic landscape can be best explored. In John Broster's *A Walk Round the Walls and City of Chester*, for example, "the traveller is [...] conducted regularly from scite to scite," escorted through a city which "merits the attention of the man of taste—claims the attention of the antiquary—and courts the admiration of the stranger."[20] Just as for visitors to Chester today, history and aesthetic charm—as well as a sense of the viewer's own discernment—converge to consolidate the appeal of the city's historic environment.

Tourist routes around Chester were well established by the late nineteenth century, when the novelist Henry James visited the city and wrote the vignettes published in *Transatlantic Sketches* (and later revised into *English Hours*). James finds Chester's built environment "prodigiously picturesque" and "a perfect feast of crookedness," and is impressed particularly by the circuit of walls which represent "an ancient property or institution, lovingly readopted and consecrated to some modern amenity."[21] James's account of his stroll through Chester is troubled throughout, however, by concerns with authenticity and the potentially fraudulent nature of the picturesque. While James presents himself as the "sentimental tourist," his friend plays the role of "cynical adversary" (p. 7), questioning the meaning and value of the quaint scenes they encounter. James himself introduces doubts regarding how far the architecture of Chester may reflect the authentic reality of its inhabitants' lives, using language laden with vocabulary of illusion and image. He finds that the picturesque scenes before him produce, for example:

> the reflection—a superficial and fallacious one, perhaps—that amid all this cunning chiaroscuro of its *mise en scène*, life must have more of a certain homely entertainment. (p. 10)

James's ambivalent attitude to Chester is shaped by his wariness of the ways in which its heritage is knowingly conserved, presented, and commodified for visitors such as himself. His concerns with "effect" and "arrangement," and the "composure" of the scenic environment (p. 12 and elsewhere), reflect his awareness of Chester's built environment as managed and mediated, both by careful civic planning and by the expectations and "fantasies" (p. 10) of the tourist. James realizes that he is unable to look through the scenic qualities of Chester, freighted with associations about the quaint character of the place and its people, to see its genuine history. Instead, for him, the landscape of Chester presents a seductive, manipulative visual rhetoric, verging on the "fatally picturesque,—horribly eloquent" (p. 13). James's language here hints at the medieval cityscape as a kind of monster:

an enchanting, unsettling hybrid of the authentic and pastiche, history and fantasy, real and staged. The spectre of the historic cityscape as a monster stalks many of the sources explored in this chapter, and is an idea to which I will return in more detail later.

Today, standing at St. John's, the impressive, majestic survival of the main church—albeit with its post-medieval alterations and additions—contrasts with the evocative, romantic medieval ruins at the east end. This juxtaposition opens up further questions about how conserved or reconstructed buildings—and, conversely, ruin and decay—speak and signify within the modern cityscape, how different kinds of built heritage are managed and presented, and the extent to which academic scholarship on the medieval city can play a positive role in the curation and interpretation of historic urban environments today. Our stroll through the streets of Chester has already revealed the city's attractive, commodified historic landscape as a series of complex hybrids and layers of historical intervention: an echo of James's picturesque monsters, which, for him, trade on a seductive, plausible aesthetics of antiquity rather than intelligible historical substance. Ruins, such as the medieval fragments of the chancel, Lady Chapel, and choir at St. John's, present different conceptual challenges. Apparently more authentic and unmediated material survivals, they are nevertheless still managed, conserved and interpreted for modern consumers. Ruins, in their own ways, invite at least as much imaginative engagement and aesthetic pleasure as the glossy fabrications of medieval buildings such as the Chester Rows: the 'feeling for ruins' from the early modern period onwards is well documented and discussed in scholarship (see Further Reading). Ruins also bring into sharp focus questions about authenticity, imagination, and licence, and the acceptable limits of material, scholarly, and creative interventions in the fabric of history.

St. John's Chester:
A Public Realm Commission

In 2011 to 2012, I was the academic / research lead for a major public realm art project at the eastern end of St. John's, which sought to curate and interpret the medieval ruins in new ways, drawing on new research on medieval Chester and its multi-lingual, multi-cultural traditions. The project was supported by twin funding streams and a range of (largely) complementary aims. Funding from the UK Arts and Humanities Research Council (AHRC) came from a "Knowledge Transfer" scheme, which promoted the dissemination of new research in innovative and imaginative ways. In this case, the findings of the inter-disciplinary, collaborative research project, "Mapping Medieval Chester" (2008–9), which explored textual and cartographic mappings of the medieval city, were the starting point for a variety of public-facing events and activities in Chester ("Discover Medieval Chester," 2012–13), of which the St. John's scheme was one element. The other, major funder of the St. John's public realm project was Cheshire West and Chester Unitary Authority (local government). The aims of the initiative at St. John's ruins included the transmission of new research insights to a wide public audience, regeneration of St. John's ruins and exploitation of the site as a previously under-used cultural asset, and creative intervention, through a new permanent public artwork, as a strategy for engaging the imagination of local communities and visitors to Chester.

The artwork was planned by local government as a proof-of-concept and pilot model for a new suite of heritage interpretation and public art policies, as well as a new public realm lighting programme, as set out in its Public Realm Strategy document (2010). This document outlines the ambitious aims of the new lighting strategy, which seeks to "assist in the development of Chester as a major tourism centre by improving the visual qualities of its night-time environment," taking "the City Walls as the unifying feature of the city's structure" and beginning with proposals for new lighting there. Overall, as stated in the Strategy document, the aspirations of the lighting programme are to:

- Unify the structure of the City by an emphasis on the lighting of the City Wall and its pathway
- Highlight the architecture and history of the City by the controlled lighting of its civic and historic buildings
- Enhance the legibility of the City by the identification of key buildings to illuminate
- Increase pedestrian use of the City by encouraging emphasis of lighting for people rather than traffic
- Expand the appreciation of the City as a visitor attraction by extending the areas of interest beyond the Walls
- Enhance the City's image by an integrated approach to lighting which combines functional, aesthetic and commercial lighting needs.[22]

For local government, the light-based artwork at St. John's was envisioned as an opportunity to enhance the medieval ruins as a previously neglected and under-exploited heritage resource (with associated potential benefits in terms of tourism and economic growth), as a way of lighting the footpath through the churchyard for pedestrians, and as a strategy to reduce anti-social behaviour in what was a dark and quiet area of the city: a complete synthesis of "functional, aesthetic and commercial" goals. The partnership between local government and the research team grounded the project in serious scholarship on medieval Chester, and presented an exciting opportunity for new research to make a real and visible intervention in today's cityscape. With an innovative, light-based artwork at its centre, the St. John's project sought to transform a neglected corner of Chester's historic cityscape in creative, engaging, and thought-provoking ways.

As a case study, the St. John's public art project illustrates the complex partnerships, cross-fertilizations, and pressures involved when a variety of stakeholders, with distinct aims and objectives, engage in the management of medieval heritage in the modern urban environment. The St. John's project returns us to questions about the imbrications, and tensions, between history, aesthetics, empiricism, and pleasure in the curation and experience of the historic cityscape. The project also presents specific questions and challenges for our understanding of the role of scholarship in interpreting the medieval cityscape. In what ways can traditional research adapt into applied and practice-led approaches which make real interventions in the urban environment? And, more broadly, when the established methods of empirical research meet creative, imaginative, and performative modes, what are the implications for our understanding of the role and value of scholarship, and its limits? Perhaps surprisingly, similar questions about empiricism, authority, imagination, and licence in the reconstruction and interpretation of the medieval past extend back into the earliest antiquarian writing from Chester, and speak powerfully to debates about heritage management—as well as wider conversations about the public role and usefulness of Humanities research—today. Even these early texts reveal anxieties about the levels of intervention acceptable when managing the historic built environment, and concerns about the role of creativity in the reconstruction (both conceptual and material) of the past. Well before Henry James's ambivalent experience of Chester in the late nineteenth century, we find the medieval cityscape stalked by disquieting monsters. Before we explore the St. John's project in more detail, let's look in detail at one of these texts and the monsters it cautions us to beware.

Heritage and Monsters

Written by an anonymous "Citizen of Chester" and printed in 1749 by Elizabeth Adams for the benefit of the city's Bluecoat School, *A Summary of the Life of St. Werburgh* takes as its starting-point the fragments of the medieval shrine of St. Werburgh in Chester Cathedral. Dismembered at the Reformation, with the relics of Werburgh removed, remnants of the fourteenth-century shrine had subsequently formed the burial place for Bishop Downham and then, from 1635, were incorporated into the new episcopal throne. The renewed interest in Werburgh's shrine represented by the Bluecoat pamphlet may well have been prompted by the partial restoration of the shrine in 1748, the year preceding the text's publication. *A Summary of the Life of St. Werburgh* comments on the recent restoration work on the surviving pieces of Werburgh's shrine, noting that its ruined state is the result of deliberate destruction rather than the gradual erosion of time.

> The Chapter of *Chester* having lately begun to beautify their Cathedral, the decayed Decorations on the Episcopal Throne engaged their Attention: This fine Piece of Antiquity had been ornamented with Carving and Statuary, both which had greatly suffered, not by Time, but by Violence: They have therefore endeavoured to repair the one, & to restore the other, so that the little IMAGES which have for so many centuries guarded, as it were, this ancient Monument, and were so injuriously defaced, are, by a commendable Care, now made whole again. (pp. 9–10)

The author's idea of the shrine "made whole again" remained a fantasy, however: after the 1748 intervention the fragments of medieval masonry continued to be used as part of the episcopal throne, and were only reconstructed in the form of a separate shrine in 1888. For the writer of the Bluecoat School pamphlet, the ruined pieces of Werburgh's shrine present a kind of metonym for Chester's early medieval past: the book seeks to reconstruct an account of the city's obscure Mercian history using the "*Images* upon Her SHRINE" (mostly representations of Anglo-Saxon kings and saints), together with details "Collected from ancient Chronicles, and old Writers" (title page). Material, scholarly, and imaginative reconstruction are closely enmeshed in this project, as a painstaking, forensic investigation of the remains of the shrine parallels a re-membering and piecing together of the Anglo-Saxon history of Chester and the Mercian kingdom. While the author acknowledges the partial, damaged, and ambiguous quality of the shrine's fragments as evidence (for example, noting that "Many of the labels [naming figures] are broke off, oth-

Figure 3. Elizabeth Adams, *A Summary of the Life of St Werburgh* (Chester, 1749), p. 9 (detail), by permission of Cheshire Archives and Local Studies

ers are so much defaced that only a Syllable or two can be read," p. 10), they are used to project narratives and gene-alogies of Mercian history. Diagrammatic representations of the carved figures and their "labels" are supplied alongside the pamphlet's text, showing clear lacunae where pieces are missing—as well as suggestions of how the intact shrine may originally have appeared.

It is the opening pages of the Bluecoat School pamphlet which speak most strikingly to wider discussions about mate-rial heritage (especially ruins) and our imaginative and schol-arly engagement with it. The *Summary of the Life of St. Wer-burgh* begins with an engraving which frames and cues the book's whole project of reconstructing and exploring the past through its material survivals.

This image depicts two gentlemen seated in a pastoral setting, surveying a picturesque ruin. The ruined façade is an ahistorical fantasy of architectural styles: an eclectic mix of classical columns, Romanesque arches and neat, rectangu-lar-style Georgian windows, which present an aesthetics of antiquity rather than any specific historical period. All these material fragments are in the process of being absorbed back into nature by the plants and trees which grow out of the crumbling stone. The two gentlemen observers are clearly in postures of leisure and repose, embodying early antiquarian-ism as a combination of private, leisured scholarship, subjec-tivity, and pleasure. Yet they are separated from the alluring ruins by a lake or river: the object of their attention remains held in the distance, inaccessible and remote. One of the gentlemen works on a sketch of the view: an artistic mode characterized by provisionality and partiality, by a creative gesture towards the perceived nature of the subject rather than a definitive, literal representation. The pamphlet's opening image thus introduces questions about how we engage with the past (and, specifically, with its traces in the built environment), including, especially, questions about the roles of pleasure and imagination and their apposition with scholarship, and the particular qualities of the ruin as the site of a pre-eminently subjective encounter with history. So far, so unsurprising: the opening engraving of the pamphlet draws on familiar eighteenth-century imagery of ruins and the picturesque to present history as an aesthetic, as much as an empirical or scholarly, construct.

But, preceding the pamphlet's engraving of the ruin and its gentlemen viewers, one other piece of paratextual content presents a more provocative, dangerous comment on our imaginative engagement with history, and material heritage specifically. The title page displays an abbreviated quotation from Ovid, which functions as an epigraph for the volume. Itself appearing as a fragment retrieved from ancient text, the quotation reads:

_____ Figuras
Retulit antiquas _____ OVID. Met.

Taken from Ovid's *Metamorphoses*, Book I, the text as excerpted might be translated as "it restored ancient forms" or perhaps more appropriately, "restoring ancient forms / shapes." This seems a wholly apt and straightforward epigraph, neatly capturing the book's project of reconstructing history—and the medieval shrine of Werburgh itself—from the ruins. However, closer attention to its context in Ovid, in a passage comparing Jupiter's great flood to the annual flooding of the Nile, suggests some more complex and provocative ideas regarding the interpretation of the "ancient forms" of material or textual fragments. Drawing on a commonplace of ancient natural history, Ovid tells us that when the waters of the Nile recede:

> plurima cultores versis animalia glaebis
> inveniunt et in his quaedam modo coepta per ipsum
> nascendi spatium, quaedam inperfecta suisque
> trunca vident numeris, et eodem in corpore saepe
> altera pars vivit, rudis est pars altera tellus.

farmers, as they turn over lumps of earth find many animate things; and among these some, but now begun, are upon the very verge of life, some are unfinished and lacking in their proper parts, and often in the same body one part is alive and the other still nothing but raw earth.[23]

He concludes by describing how, after the great flood, the earth:

> edidit innumeras species; partimque figures
> retulit antiquas, partim nova monstra creavit.

brought forth innumerable forms of life; in part restoring ancient shapes, and in part creating new monsters.

(lines 436–37)

While Ovid celebrates the generative, creative power of the Nile floods—and especially their ability to restore life to the dead earth—he also alludes to the potential of this restorative process to exceed or transgress the limits of what has gone before. Indeed, the classical image of the Nile flood is used with a specifically textual meaning in Book I of Spenser's *Faerie Queene*, where it becomes a metaphor for dangerous, excessive reading and the misappropriation or perversion of texts. Choked by the Redcrosse Knight, Error's vomit of books and papers—and her "inky" children—is compared to the flood of the Nile which leaves "Such ugly monstrous shapes elswhere may no man reed."[24] Spenser's text offers a precedent for linking the image of the Nile flood to the dangers of interpretation and the (re)construction of meaning. While *A Summary of the Life of St. Werburgh* edits its epigraph carefully, excising the more ambivalent elements of the Ovid passage, the troubling implications of its source context encroach on the text. "Figuras / retulit antiquas" is a brave ideal of regeneration out of recovered fragments and partial survivals. But it also gestures towards the possibilities of distortion, deformation, and even the creation of unsanctioned, chimeric forms. Unspoken monsters haunt the Bluecoat School pamphlet, recalling Henry James's sense of the unnerving picturesque of Chester's re-modelled medieval cityscape, or the most troubling excesses of interventionist modern "restoration" projects. Must the conservation or reconstruction of "ancient forms" always precipitate the creation of "new monsters"? And in what ways might this speak to projects which seek to manage the material fabric of the medieval city today? Is the historic cityscape always, inevitably, a monster?

St. John's Public Artwork

The public realm project at St. John's, Chester, used light as the medium for its intervention in the physical environment, limiting its material impact on the fabric of the medieval ruins and their immediate context. The light-based artwork, while permanent, was designed so that it can be removed easily if required in the future, without damaging the historic site. The commissioned artist, Nayan Kulkarni, brought extensive experience in creating site-specific artworks, and particularly installations based on illumination and light projection. His catalogue features works such as *Cascade* (2008), on the site of the former mill race by the Silk Museum, Derby, which uses ground-based light projections suggesting the movement of water across mill races, and *Mirrie Dancers* (2007 onwards), a series of temporary installations in the Shetland Islands, which include the projection of light through Shetland lace onto buildings. The finished installation at St. John's is based on LED project systems using specially fabricated glass slides (similar to theatrical gobos) which are focused on the medieval ruins using cinema lenses. Each slide is an image no larger than fifty millimetres in diameter, including both fac-

Figure 4. Nayan Kulkarni, *Hryre* (2012), St John's Ruins, Chester. Photo by Nayan Kulkarni.

simile images taken from medieval manuscripts and excerpts of medieval texts from and about Chester in modern type-face (see Figure 4 and the following discussion). The dynamic projection cycle—in which patterns of brightness, projected images, and timings vary—is controlled by a computer pro-gram, with Easter as its fulcrum, when the greatest number of projections display and converge.

As a permanent artwork, the installation is required to function for at least twenty-five years; the build quality and material choices mean that the technical infrastructure of the artwork can be reconditioned as lamp technology chan-ges. The artwork thus makes a very visible, and potentially very long-lasting, intervention in the cityscape at St. John's Church, without substantial material modification to the ruins themselves. But, even as a light-based work, the installation at St. John's required a degree of environmental interven-tion and alteration, including, most controversially, removing plants which had overgrown much of the site. This transfor-mation was met with concern by some local people: as in the engraving at the start of the Chester Bluecoat Pamphlet, the imagery of picturesque ruins enveloped in encroaching greenery clearly still holds imaginative power as a signifier of a distant, romanticized past. Interestingly, according to some perspectives, the overgrown greenery at St. John's was as integral to the site's historic character as the medieval stone ruins themselves, raising familiar questions about the role of selectivity and subjectivity in determining which elements of the cityscape are worthy of preservation and protection. The St. John's artwork, then, illustrates the significant changes (for better or worse) which can be made to the aesthetics and meanings of a heritage site within the cityscape, even without direct alteration to the surviving historic fabric itself.

I collaborated with the commissioned artist, Nayan Kulkarni, on the development of the St. John's artwork, having previously led the research project "Mapping Medieval Chester," which informed this new interpretation of the city's medieval heritage. Our aim was for the light projections to represent the rich, complex history of Chester as a borderland city (on the boundary between England and Wales) in the Middle Ages. In particular, we hoped to make visible to a wider public the rich literary heritage of medieval Chester: the surviving texts which imagine and describe the city from varying cultural and ethnic perspectives. The "Mapping Medieval Chester" project focused on texts which we have already encountered in our walk through Chester's medieval cityscape: *De Laude Cestrie*, written by Lucian (probably a monk at St. Werburgh's) in the late twelfth century; the Middle English verse *Life of St. Werburge*, by Henry Bradshaw, also a monk at St. Werburgh's, dating to the early sixteenth century; Ranulph Higden's poem to Chester from his *Polychronicon* (mid fourteenth century); and a range of late-medieval vernacular Welsh poems relating to Chester, including satire and invective targeted at the city as a site of English colonial rule, as well as devotional poetry inspired by the relics of the True Cross at St. John's Church (see www.medievalchester.ac.uk). Selecting excerpts from the medieval texts for inclusion in the artwork was a collaborative, consultative process involving workshops with community groups and stakeholders such as local government, schools, Chester's Grosvenor Museum, and the Diocese of Chester (the St. John's ruins site remains consecrated ground and under the authority of the Church of England).

The shifting illuminations and combinations produced by the artwork's computer-controlled projection program offer an opportunity to visualize the exchanges, tensions, and collisions which characterized the culture of Chester as a borderland city in the Middle Ages. The light-based artwork places fragments from different texts in provocative juxta-position and intersection, as words in Middle English, Latin, and Welsh emerge, converge, and disappear. For example, excerpts from Lucian's encomium to Chester and Henry Brad-shaw's panegyric descriptions of the city in his *Life of St. Werburge* overlap with the satirical vitriol of Lewys Glyn Cothi's "Dychan I Wŷr o Gaer" ("Satire on the Men of Chester"), in which the speaker declares that "oerchwedl i'r dinas mewn dwfr bas bach" ("I seek vengeance on the city in its shallow little water," l. 30). Through its projections of medieval texts over the fourteenth-century ruins, the artwork finds an inno-vative way of connecting Chester's intangible cultural her-itage to the tangible heritage of its material environment. While the projection texts are in their original medieval lan-guages, interpretation and glosses are available in St. John's Church and online. However, the medieval character of the manuscript facsimile images are recognizable to most casual visitors, as, for many people, are the languages themselves (in broad character, even if not intelligible: English, Latin, and Welsh) and their wider cultural and historical associations. Thus, the artwork begins to find ways to make visible the social, cultural, and political landscapes of medieval Chester, alongside its surviving material cityscape.

Central to the final artwork at St. John's—an emphasis developed through discussion with local people as well as through my partnership with the artist—are the themes of ruin, decay, and survival. Indeed, the title of the artwork, cho-sen by Nayan Kulkarni, is *Hryre*, the Old English word for "fall" or "ruin." Taking its thematic imperatives from the site itself, the installation explores ideas of loss and endurance through relevant excerpts from the medieval texts, which themselves show concerns with history and transience. A passage from Henry Bradshaw's *Life of St. Werburge* recalls the supposed destruction brought by a terrible fire sometime in the late twelfth century, comparing Chester to the great ruined cities of antiquity.

> Alas, great heuyness it was to beholde
> The cite of Troye all flaming as fire:
> More pite of Rome city was manyfolde,
> Feruently flagrant / empeiryng the empire:
> As to quantite, the cite of Chestire
> Myght be assembled this tyme in like case
> To the sayd citees, remedelees, alas!
>
> (lines 1626–32)

Ranulph Higden's description of Chester's mighty walls as "velut Hercules actus" ("like a deed of Hercules") takes on a hubristic, melancholy resonance when projected across the crumbling stonework at St. John's. References to the tide ("llanw") gleaned from Welsh poetry (referring to the miraculous sea-borne arrival of the relics of the True Cross at St. John's) and storms ("tempestas") in Lucian's *De Laude Cestrie* convey a sense of the patterns and vicissitudes of passing time. Excerpts such as these, which point to transience and decay, are set against others which suggest survival, renewal and recovery. Maredudd ap Rhys's poem "I'r Groes or Gaer" ("To the Cross at Chester") recalls Christ's miracle which brought "Lasar o fol ddaear dud" ("Lazarus from the belly of the black earth," l. 50). Lucian, as we saw in our walk to St. John's, sets the secular busyness of the castle against the eternal concerns of St. John's and the "solatio" or "tranquillitas" it offers. And even Lewys Glyn Cothi's stinging satire, calling down curses on the men of Chester, provides the words "ond yr eglwysau yn dir glasach" ("but let the churches stay in a greener land," l. 44), reflecting reverence and affection for the ecclesiastical and spiritual sites of the city. Displayed in both typeset text and manuscript facsimile on the

St. John's ruins, this phrase speaks of the special status of Chester's medieval churches as sites of veneration and devotion for centuries, and suggests, with its echoes of pastoral "greenness," the possibility of an Edenic world beyond the contamination of time, corruption, and decay (the lack of a verb in the Welsh here further reinforces the sense of an aspiration beyond and outside of time). Fittingly, then, the St. John's artwork brings together medieval perspectives on the history of Chester, as well as broader reflections on questions of transience, loss, and endurance, in this modern installation which seeks to manage and interpret a fragmentary survival of the medieval cityscape.

The medieval texts displayed in the light projections at St. John's indicate that concerns with the material traces of the past—and their meanings for viewers in the present—are not new. The site of St. John's ruins itself has, in the past two centuries, inspired a substantial body of art and literature which looks back to an imagined medieval past and reflects on themes of transience, loss, and endurance. The picturesque scene of St. John's ruins, crumbling and overgrown with foliage, was a favourite subject of nineteenth-century engravers in Chester. These images all delight in the juxtaposition between culture and nature, with the collapsing stonework and encroaching trees and plants emblematic of the transience of human life and the passing of time. A lithograph of "St. John's Church and Priory, Chester" by W. Tasker, in the collection of Chester Library, even juxtaposes the conventional scene of the medieval ruins with a funeral procession leaving the north door of the church and a woman in mourning at a graveside in the foreground. Such an obvious use of St. John's ruins as a *memento mori* calls attention to the susceptibility of the ruin to moralising or didactic interpretations and uses. Indeed, nineteenth-century depictions of St. John's are not merely based on aesthetic or sentimental responses, but also make use of the ruins to speak to cultural and political concerns. A "Historical Account," privately printed as a pamphlet by the Rev. Francis Grosvenor in 1857 and now in the collection of the Cheshire Record Office, brings together the aesthetic, moral, and political potentials of the ruins. The author comments that "It will [...] be deemed excusable if the archaeologist, who delights to search out and preserve the relics of past greatness, lingers over the beautiful remains of this fabric in admiration of its departed grandeur, and with a feeling of regret for its present dilapidated condition." He adds that this "amusement" may be blended with "usefulness," allowing the viewer "to draw from the experience of the past, instruction for the present, or guidance for the future" (p. 3). For Grosvenor, the ruins represent more troubling potentials alongside the past "greatness" of his country: he describes the destructive forces of the Reformation as "barbarism" and deplores "the rapacity of the covetous, and the bigotry of religious zealots" (p. 4). Grosvenor reads the medieval ruins at St. John's as a warning against the evils of extremism: the antithesis of his mid-Victorian values of conservatism, tradition, and continuity.

Varying interpretations of the ruins at St. John's Church remind us of the ways in which the historic cityscape can be freighted with aesthetic, moral, and even political values. While the picturesque appeal of Chester's conserved and restored medieval (or quasi-medieval) architecture invites ready imaginative connection with the past, more fragmentary survivals, such as the ruins at St. John's, attract perhaps an even more intensely subjective engagement with history and our relationship to it. As the historian Sophie Thomas observes, responses to ruins always reveal "the historical relation, rather than history 'itself'."[25] Of course, engagement with and management of the historic cityscape in all its forms—whether intact or fragmentary—reveals the concerns and attitudes of the present as much as any authentic historical truths. Curation of the historic built environment always results in processes of renewal, reproduction, and re-making. As we have seen, commentators such as Henry James and the author of the Chester Bluecoat Pamphlet are among the early voices warning that such interventions—whether material or merely interpretative—may conjure "new monsters" out of the remnants of history. Concerns about the danger of inventing hybrid monsters of history and fantasy were particularly acute and pertinent in the development of the artwork at St. John's ruins. The project offered an opportunity for academic research to directly inform an intervention in the historic cityscape, and for a key public realm project to be securely grounded in the latest historical scholarship. But the St. John's initiative also provoked questions about what kinds of activity or intervention might be accommodated within notions of scholarship and scholarly practice, and about the limits of scholarly inquiry and methodology. What happens when research meets creative practice within the urban landscape?

Research and Creative Practice

Producing the St. John's artwork involved creative interventions and interpolations which moved well beyond the typical remit of analytical, critical scholarly inquiry. While the material fabric of the stone ruins at St. John's was left largely untouched, the textual and cultural fabric of literature from medieval Chester was appropriated and manipulated in profound ways. The collage approach of the artwork involved taking apart medieval texts and reassembling their fragments into new contexts, inferring new meanings and emphases from the original sources. The thematic focus of *Hryre* meant foregrounding content from the medieval texts which related to subjects of time, ruin and survival—all, as we have seen, touched upon in the literature, but never the primary subject of the material. These are texts which we ourselves have deliberately fragmented in order to produce the artwork, breaking words away from their original locations and presenting them instead as shards gathered into new configurations and meanings. In some ways, this process enacts the "pleasure of ruins" on the texts themselves, with the "looting, carrying away of fragments" replacing the more conventional methodologies of scholarly editing and analysis.[26] The recuperative process of gathering and re-assembling textual fragments also presents a suggestive parallel with the practices involved, historically, in re-building and restoring historic architecture—with all the dangers of "new monsters" inherent in those projects. Significantly, our feedback from local people in Chester (gathered by survey and text message service) suggested that the fragmentary nature of the medieval texts projected at St. John's appealed to viewers: their allusive, partial character reinforced and satisfied popular notions of the Middle Ages as a cultural space of mystery, incompleteness and ambiguity. Yet the fragments were of our own making, serving the objectives of a contemporary art project.

It would be naïve to suggest that academic methods and priorities would—or should—remain unchanged when drawn into collaborative enterprise with other, more creative practices, or when brought to bear on specific, applied problems and contexts—such as the regeneration of the St. John's ruins site. The St. John's project showed clearly that when academic research meets public interpretation and engagement, the parameters of conventional scholarly activity require recalibration. The broader implications of this are more significant than has often been acknowledged. Of course, new research has the capacity to inform and transform practice-led and applied projects within the urban environment (and more widely). But partnership working, creative collaborations, and applied or performative modes also bring the potential—indeed, the inevitability—of change to established academic methodologies. While discourses of "public engagement" and "impact" gain increasing traction in debates about the public role and value of the Humanities, little attention has been paid to the ways in which these in which these potentials—even priorities—may change the nature of what we recognize as Humanities scholarship. The methods of the St. John's art project included manipulating medieval texts in ways which transgressed the conventionally-acceptable limits of scholarly engagement and analysis. The development of the artwork interposed creative, performative, and imaginative modes alongside more familiar critical idioms, moving beyond the kind of discourse and output usually licensed by empirical authority. The challenges of re-conceptualizing the role and ambit—and limitations—of scholarship in relation to public practice bring us back to questions of ambition, adventure, and the putative monsters lurking on the way. In the final section of this chapter, I want to return to a long-view exploration of discourses surrounding the medieval cityscape in Chester and its management. Such an overview calls attention once again to questions about the curation of built heritage—whether largely intact or in the form of ruins—and the imbricated, complementary, sometimes strained relationships between imagination, creativity, and scholarship in its interpretation. Two texts from Chester, Daniel King's *Vale-Royall of England* (Chester, 1656) and W.P. Greswell's *The Monastery of St. Werburgh: A Poem with Illustrative Notes* (Manchester: privately printed, 1823), deal with these questions in contrasting ways.

The Vale-Royall of England, or, The County Palatine of Chester begins with an anonymous poem both in Latin and "Englished," addressed to King as compiler and renovator of the county's history. The Latin verses begin with repeated exhortations to Chester: "Cestria tolle caput" ("Chester, lift your head") and again "tolle" ("rise"), calling the city to lift itself from the tomb of ruin and decay ("sepulchro," given in the English as "urne") and assert its noble heritage as "Brutigenae [...] gloria terrae" (translated as "Glory of the British Isle"). The English verses go on to form an effusive panegyric to King, celebrating his work restoring the history of the city and Palatinate.

> What Guerdon shall thy studious Reader give
> Thee, KING! by whom these Monuments do live?
> For had they not been Thus preserv'd, we must
> Have left those Trophies groveling in the dust:
> But Thou dispell'st those Clouds, and do'st restore
> That pristine Beauty which they had before [...]
>
> (p. 18)

The "Monuments" restored by King in *The Vale-Royall* include textual artefacts—documentary evidence and material from old books—and the metaphorical edifices of the city's history, recovered through study and scholarship. But, prominently, they also include the material heritage of Chester, catalogued and described in detail in substantial sections of *The Vale-Royall*, such as William Webb's imagined ambulation around the city's streets. While drawing on material metaphors of reconstruction and renewal, the poem proclaims the potential of "th'elaborate Pen"—the authorial and textual project of King and his contributors—to recover the glory of Chester's "Monuments." The opening verses thus make an emphatic and significant statement. It is not only physical, material intervention, and rebuilding which can rescue the historic cityscape, but also the power of scholarship (here firmly rooted in antiquarian and chorographic traditions), textual representation, and interpretation. The vision of the poem is supremely optimistic and idealistic: the ensuing text of *The Vale-Royall* will save "those Trophies grovelling in the dust," restoring them to "That pristine Beauty which they had before." The poem imagines and promises a perfect, exact reproduction of Chester's heritage—no less and no more, and with no hint of the monsters of imaginative excess, error, or unauthorized interpolation hovering in the shadows. The only touch of ambivalence or ambiguity here might be the double meaning of the Latin verb *tollere* ("to rise, lift; to destroy, remove"), which might, perhaps unintentionally, hint at the precariousness of any process of restoration. King's *Vale-Royall of England* is announced as a perfect, pure project of restoration to "pristine," authentic originals—albeit in the form of textual and artistic representations, rather than in the material environment itself.

W. P. Greswell's long poem *The Monastery of St. Werburgh*, printed in Manchester in 1823, presents a different and more ambivalent position in relation to history, the medieval cityscape and its material or textual recovery. The poem offers a dramatized history of medieval Chester, prompted by a walk through the medieval cloisters of the city's cathedral, formerly the Abbey of St. Werburgh. The first stanza introduces the site and the suggestive dilapidation of the medieval architecture.

Lo! where triumphant o'er the wreck of years
The time-worn Fabrick lifts its awful [awe-inspiring] form:
Scath'd with the blast its sculptur'd front appears,
Yet frowns defiance on the impetuous storm.
What Pow'rs—to more than giant bulk ally'd,
Thy firm-compacted mass conspir'd to raise!
Then bade thee stand secure to latest days,
Wonder of after times,—of Cestria's sires the pride.

(p. 1)

Recalling the leisured contemplation depicted in the opening engraving of the Bluecoat School pamphlet, the poem's
narrator confesses that "I—solitary—love to linger here" (p.
3), among the material relics and traces of history. From out
of the crumbling fabric of the cathedral and its cloisters, St.
Werburgh appears as a ghostly guide to both the narrator
and a young minstrel depicted within the narrative. She
beckons them out of "Conjecture's labyrinth" and presents
a "fleeting pageant" (p. 8) of ghostly characters associated
with St. Werburgh's through the Middle Ages, from "Saxon
Maids" to Hugh Lupus and Chester's other medieval Earls, to
Benedictine monks and festive pilgrims.

It seems that Greswell's poem was composed partly as
a response to a recent programme of restoration and reconstruction of the medieval architecture at St. Werburgh's in
the early nineteenth century. The poem's first explanatory
note (glossing the line "Scath'd with the blast its sculptur'd
front appears") comments that "[m]ore than thirty years have
elapsed, since the Author first sketched the rude outline of
the POEM which after various corrections and additions is now
submitted to the Public." In this time, the author continues,
the graceful decay of the cathedral's fabric had "become so
ruinous as to require speedy measures to arrest (at least in
some degree) the rapid process of dilapidation." Greswell
goes on:

Very recently several parts of the exterior have been
restored by a new casing—and others are now undergoing
a like process. At present therefore, the sacred Pile no longer wears its late uniform aspect of decay; but the eye is

> somewhat offended by an incongruous mixture of recent and antique. (p. 25)

Greswell is unsettled by this composite of medieval and modern, acknowledging the "regret of the antiquary" (p. 26) when the original fabric of a structure is modified and compromised. He notes, also, that certain material features ("appendages") of the medieval monastery have been removed altogether, "either for want of funds for their reparation, or in compliance with suggestions of modern convenience" (p. 26). Indeed, Greswell claims that some of the atmospheric scenes of ancient survival and picturesque decay described in his poem are now no longer recognizable at the cathedral site—though his verses still exploit the imagery of the romantic ruin as an imaginative conduit to the past. Having written the poem so many years previously, if his claims are true, then Greswell's publication of *The Monastery of St. Werburgh* in 1823 can be understood in part as a reaction to—and against—the recent renovation of St. Werburgh's and its impact on the historic environment of the cathedral and its precincts.

The material reconstruction of St. Werburgh's is not the only focus of Greswell's ambivalence and anxiety in *The Monastery of St. Werburgh*. His own project of bringing to life the medieval environment and history of the cathedral cloisters— his textual intervention in the historic cityscape—is fraught with disquiet. The poem is accompanied by a substantial paratext, which takes up twenty-three of the volume's forty-eight pages. A familiar feature of much literature in this period, Greswell's paratextual notes nevertheless express particular concerns and divided commitments, which underlie the production of the poem. Greswell sustains a dual, or parallel, discourse throughout the text, using these detailed historical notes at the end of the poem to license and sanction the imaginative flourishes of the verse. The poem maintains its authority and value as an antiquarian text only through the presence of the scholarly paratext, which includes citation of scholarly sources and discussion of history, specific historical figures, and the text of the Benedictine Rule. For example, two women appear alongside Werburgh:

Each in her hand a flickering taper bore,
That shed faint lustre through the dim abode:
Sable [black], their robes descending swept the floor;
A snowy veil adown each bosom flow'd. (p. 9)

Interpreting the scene, St. Werburgh identifies the figures only briefly as "Milburg and Mildred lov'd—of Woden sprung [...] my kindred vestals they" (p. 9). The explanatory end notes, however, give detailed historical background on these figures and the genealogy of the Mercian royal line (p. 30), drawn partly from the study of the iconography of Werburgh's shrine, which appears in the Bluecoat pamphlet, discussed above. Similarly, Werburgh reveals "Visions long past" as the medieval splendour of the abbey church is displayed to the minstrel and the poem's narrator, while the notes give a detailed account of the monastery buildings and their later uses (pp. 14, 37).

The dual structure of *The Monastery of St. Werburgh* calls attention to a tension at the heart of the work. Creative, imaginative processes and idioms provide Greswell's route into history and the means of its recuperation and representation in the verse. Yet the detailed, meticulously referenced scholarly paratext betrays an unease with the value and authority of imagination as a mode of inquiry, and a need to regulate and police the more creative energies of the text. Greswell's work emerges as a strange, uncomfortable hybrid, every bit as much as the restored medieval architecture of St. Werburgh's which disquiets him so evidently. Greswell's textual reconstruction of the medieval cityscape is fraught with concerns about authority, empirical evidence, and the legitimacy of creative idioms: his structural approach to these concerns is his attempt to guard against the "monsters" potentially generated when imagination meets scholarship in the recuperation of the historic urban environment.

Scholarship, the Medieval Cityscape, and the Public Realm

Our exploration of Chester has raised a range of questions about the nature of the medieval cityscape today and our relationships with it. We have considered some of the ways in which we engage with medieval built heritage—whether the compelling completeness of restored or remodelled buildings, or the suggestive possibilities presented by ruins. We have seen some of the different kinds of intervention possible or appropriate in the management and interpretation of the medieval cityscape, from physical reconstruction to less invasive methods, and with reference to intangible as well as tangible cultural heritage. We have examined the inter-locking and sometimes strained relationships between scholarship, imagination and creative practice in informing and delivering these interventions. And we have begun to think about ways in which academic research can make a contribution to and have a stake in the curation of the historic urban environment. Our route through the medieval cityscape of Chester has also brought us into proximity with the monsters which prowl projects of restoration, reconstruction, and re-development. They haunt Henry James's encounter with the "fatally picturesque,—horribly eloquent" scenes of Chester in the late nineteenth century, and his troubling sense of sleight of hand, illusion, and trickery. They are suppressed but still powerful in the Ovidian epigraph to the Bluecoat School pamphlet's reconstruction of Werburgh's shrine and early Chester history, with its warning that the renewal of "ancient forms" can easily generate "new monsters." In the dedicatory verse to Daniel King's *Vale-Royall of Chester* we find instead an optimistic—but impossible—fantasy of the restoration of authentic "pristine Beauty." And in Greswell's *The Monastery of St. Werburgh* we see tensions between scholarly conservatism and creative excess played out in the verse and accompanying paratext. These historical sources introduce concerns and anxieties which remain profound today, and which continue to influence debates about the treatment of built heritage in the urban environment, as well as its public interpretation. The texts we have examined, from King to James, show that questions about licence, legitimacy, and authority are not new, but present and insistent from the earliest antiquarian writing.

Many of these questions and concerns converge in the case study of the public realm project at St. John's ruins. The St. John's artwork, with its light-based installation, suggested one approach to redeveloping and renewing a site within the medieval cityscape without disruptive material interventions, and experimented with approaches to bringing together tangible (built) and intangible (cultural) heritage in visible and accessible ways. However, while respecting the integrity of the material fabric of the ruins at St. John's Church, the methods of the project opened up their own risks of 'new monsters'. The development of the artwork took us beyond the limits of conventional academic practice, into more creative, interventionist, and manipulative treatment of the medieval texts selected for projection. The project underlined the rich opportunities for academic research to engage with creative practitioners and planners in the development of the urban environment. Yet it also demonstrated the impact of such collaborations on traditional scholarly methods, and their implications for making "new monsters" out of the established norms of academic practice.

The St. John's art project encourages us to think optimistically about the capacity of academic research to make positive interventions in the urban environment, and urges us to enlarge our definition of scholarship to include more creative, practice-based and experimental modes. While the antiquarian and historiographical texts examined in this chapter—from Daniel King to Henry James—have given us the idea of "ancient forms" and "new monsters" as provocative tools to think with, now is the right time to discard and move beyond the notion of monsters in the medieval cityscape and its interpretation. The image of the monster implies a dichotomy between the original and its reproduction, deformation, or corruption, presenting the medieval cityscape today as a realm of troubling, inauthentic hybrids. Instead, in sites such as the Rows of Chester, the city's Eastgate, or the precincts of St. Werburgh's, we find a rich, multi-layered urban environment which embodies centuries of revision, renewal, and re-making. While acknowledging the importance of protecting historic features and landscapes, it is also possible to embrace the historic cityscape as a document of continual and continuing change. Sloughing off some of our fear of monsters opens up possibilities for more playful, creative, and experimental exchanges and dialogues within the urban environment: between eras and architectures, and between academics and the city.

Notes

[7] William Smith, extract from *The Particuler Description of England With The Portratures of Certaine the Chieffest Citties and Townes*, collected in *The Vale-Royall of England, or, The County Palatine of Chester, performed by William Smith, and William Webb, Gentlemen* (Chester: Daniel King, 1656), 40.

[8] *A History of the County of Chester*, vol. 5:ii, "Major Buildings: The Rows," in *The City of Chester: Culture, Buildings, Institutions*, ed. A. T. Thacker and C. P. Lewis (Woodbridge: Published for the Institute of Historical Research by Boydell & Brewer, 2005), 225–39. Other chapters of this volume are cited below.

[9] S. W. Ward, "The Archaeology of Medieval Chester: A Review," *Journal of the Chester Archaeological Society* 73 (1994–5): 31–62 at 50.

[10] Tony Haskell, *Caring for Our Built Heritage: Conservation in Practice* (London: Taylor and Francis, 2006), 150.

[11] For this claim, see "A Virtual Stroll Around the Walls of Chester" (https://www.chesterwalls.info/eastgate.html).

[12] "Major Buildings: City Walls and Gates," in *The City of Chester: Culture, Buildings, Institutions, 213–25*.

[13] Lucian, *De Laude Cestrie*, ed. and trans. Mark Faulkner, fol. 12r. All quotations from *De Laude Cestrie* are taken from www.medievalchester.ac.uk.

[14] John Speed, *The Theatre of the Empire of Great Britaine, presenting an exact geography of the Kingdomes of England, Scotland, Ireland and the Iles adioyning* (London: J. Sudbury and G. Humble, 1611).

[15] Ranulph Higden, *A Poem to Chester*, ed. and trans. Helen Fulton (www.medievalchester.ac.uk), lines 3, 5, 15–16.

[16] "Churches and Religious Bodies: The Collegiate Church of St John," in *The City of Chester: Culture, Buildings, Institutions*, 125–33.

[17] Henry Bradshaw, *The Life of St Werburge*, ed. Catherine A. M. Clarke (www.medievalchester.ac.uk), lines 1179, 1180.

[18] Barry J. Lewis, *Welsh Poetry and English Pilgrimage: Gruffudd ap Maredudd and the Rood of Chester* (Aberystwyth: University of Wales, Centre for Advanced Welsh and Celtic Studies, 2005), 20.

[19] David Mills, "Chester Ceremonial: Re-creation and Recreation in the English 'Medieval' Town," *Urban History* 18 (1991): 1–19 at 7.

[20] John Broster, *A Walk Round the Walls and City of Chester* (Chester: John Broster, 1821), i, 91.

[21] Henry James, *Transatlantic Sketches* (Boston: James R. Osgood, 1875), 11, 10, 8.

[22] *Public Realm Strategy, Four: Arts, Lighting and Wayfaring Strategy* (Chester: Cheshire West and Chester Council, 2009), 42.

[23] Ovid, *Metamorphoses*, with an English translation by Frank Justis Miller, 2 vols. (Cambridge, MA: Harvard University Press, 1951), vol. 1, bk. II, lines 425–29, 32–33.

[24] Spenser, *The Faerie Queene*, ed. A. C. Hamilton (London: Longman, 1989), Book I, Canto i, verse 21.

[25] Sophie Thomas, *Romanticism and Visuality: Fragments, History, Spectacle* (New York: Routledge, 2008), 50.

[26] See Rose Macaulay's seminal discussion *Pleasure of Ruins*, 2nd ed. (New York: Walker, 1967), xvi.

Chapter 2

Swansea: Seeing the Invisible City— Spatial Encounters Past and Present

This chapter asks questions about how we might begin to recover and interpret lost or absent medieval cityscapes, and models possible approaches through the digital and material strategies which formed elements of the "City Witness" research project in Swansea.

Dylan Thomas Comes Home

In his short radio play *Return Journey*, commissioned by the BBC and broadcast in 1947, poet Dylan Thomas describes a visit to his childhood home of Swansea, just a few years after the devastation of wartime air raids on the town. Thomas evokes the bombed landscape of Swansea on a cold February day: its "vanished buildings," the "blitzed flat graves of shops," and the "havoc'd" town centre.[27] He walks along High Street:

> [...] past the flat white wastes where all the shops had been. Eddershaw Furnishers, Curry's Bicycles, Donegal Clothing Company, Doctor Scholl's, Burton Tailors, W.H. Smith, Boots Cash Chemists, Leslie's Stores, Upson's Shoes, Prince of Wales, Tucker's Fish, Stead & Simpson—all the shops bombed and vanished. Past the hole in space where Hodges & Clothiers had been, down Castle Street, past the remembered, invisible shops [...] (pp. 105-6)

Thomas's careful catalogue of absence continues; his faithful recitation of the names of lost, disappeared shops and landmarks forming a solemn reckoning of the town's destruction. Later, recounting his walk along College Street, Thomas uses the same phrase, once more listing the "remembered invisible shops" which he can still imagine in the midst of the ruined urban landscape (p. 111). The "ugly, lovely" pre-war town, described so tenderly in Thomas's *Reminiscences of Childhood*,[28] has vanished, its buildings "melted" into nothing (p. 114). Yet Thomas still sees each of these familiar landmarks in his mind's eye: he assembles their names into their former rows and sequences along streets; into the remembered narratives of itineraries through the vanished town centre. For Thomas, the Swansea of his childhood is still visible, and present, even amongst the "snow and ruin" of the blitzed streets (p. 108).

Dylan Thomas's personal account of this catastrophic rupture in the landscape and history of Swansea presents another way into thinking about medieval cityscapes today, and especially the challenges and opportunities involved in engaging with lost or "invisible" historic environments. This chapter takes Swansea as a case study for exploring these ideas: a city with a rich and fascinating medieval history, but where the historic material landscape is now mostly invisible, in large part due to the wartime bomb damage which Thomas so vividly describes. The idea of the invisible city will connect my approach to the urban landscape of Swansea in the Middle Ages, and surviving evidence for the spatial practices of its inhabitants, with my discussion of strategies for interpreting and engaging with the unseen medieval heritage of Swansea today. I will examine the invisible social and cultural geographies which operate within the medieval town, as well as ways in which the historic town is encoded invisibly within the present-day urban environment and how, in the absence of material traces, we might be able to understand and experience these hidden realms and strata within the physical landscape. My discussion will also identify and critique some of the contrasting discourses, in particular those emerging from heritage practice and critical theory, which articulate, in very different ways, the relationships between the city, history, and memory, and the ways in which the past can be experienced through place.

In this chapter, I build on new research on medieval Swansea funded by the UK Arts and Humanities Research Council as part of the project "City Witness: Place and Perspective in Medieval Swansea" (www.medievalswansea.ac.uk). This inter-disciplinary, collaborative research project explored place and identity within this town in the medieval Marches (the border region between England and Wales, controlled in the Middle Ages by Anglo-Norman lords), linking new mappings of Swansea ca. 1300 with contemporary accounts of itineraries and experiences within the medieval urban landscape. The project also produced a footpath ("pavement") marker series, linked to interactive, multi-media interpretation resources, designed to re-connect the city of Swansea today with its (largely invisible) medieval past, and to engage modern communities with its rich medieval heritage. This process of making the invisible historic landscape of Swansea visible once again, of re-inscribing an absent or unseen geography within the modern city streets, raises compelling questions about the relationships between material and invisible urban landscapes in both the modern city and its medieval antecedent.

In this chapter, I will pursue the critical opportunities and challenges presented by the Swansea research and pavement marker project, thinking through the conceptual and theoretical implications of what it means to witness the invisible city. How can we recover the invisible cultural and social landscapes of medieval Swansea itself, which leave so little in terms of material fabric? What are the particular challenges—and perhaps opportunities—for interpreting medieval heritage in a location like Swansea, where so much is now lost or visually absent? And what are the limits of visualization and seeing as a route into engagement with the past? The pavement marker project translated the "City Witness" research on medieval Swansea into the realm of public heritage interpretation, in which the dominant practical discourse is predicated on notions of continuity, contiguity, and recognizable, perceptible connection with the past. But can experiences of disjunction, dislocation, and estrangement—such as those presented by attempts to discover Swansea's medieval heritage within the post-war city—form equally powerful routes into imaginative engagement? Finally, can we bring together the divergent assumptions and discourses associated with heritage practice and scholarly research / critical theory on the city, in order to extend and nuance our understanding of medieval cityscapes and their interpretation today? I will conclude the chapter with a short study of a specific place in Swansea, Wassail Square, exploring its curious, ambivalent blend of invisibility and endurance from the Middle Ages to the present day; its susceptibility to slipping off the map, yet its persistence in memory and imagination. My detailed analysis of Wassail Square will bring the chapter's central themes and questions into sharp focus, through the biography of one particular location within the cityscape and its visible and invisible lives.

Material and Cultural Geographies in Medieval Swansea

Evidence for the early history and urban development of Swansea is fragmentary and problematic, compounded by the fact that so little of the material fabric and street pattern of the medieval town survive today. Conventional accounts of the town's history present it as an Anglo-Norman plantation town in the marcher lordship of Gower, though there is some evidence from both urban morphology and the etymology of its name (usually interpreted as deriving from "Sweynes-ey" or "the island of Sveinn") for earlier Viking origins (see Further Reading). The first Norman castle was built in 1116, with the "New" Castle constructed ca. 1284–90; other features of the early Anglo-Norman town include the parish church of St. Mary and the market located just to south of the castle bailey at the top of Wind Street. Archaeological excavations in Swansea during the later twentieth century revealed evidence of lost medieval defences (walls and ditches) as well as sites of occupation reaching back to the twelfth century. These excavations and their varying interpretations led to a range of mappings of medieval Swansea, including Edith Evans's detailed "conjectural plan of Swansea about 1400" and subsequent re-assessments by local archaeologists in the early twenty-first century.[29] As part of the "City Witness" project, Keith Lilley and Gareth Dean produced a map of Swansea ca. 1300, building on the methodology of using GIS (Geographical Information Systems) for mapping medieval townscapes first developed by Lilley in his earlier project "Mapping the Medieval Urban Landscape: Edward I's New Towns of England and Wales" and later used in the "Mapping Medieval Chester" project.[30] Using this approach, Lilley and Dean drew together evidence gathered from all previous archaeological investigations into medieval Swansea, as well as interpretations derived from retrogressive plan analysis and documentary sources, to produce both an interactive digital atlas and a static map of the town ca. 1300, which, though still far from conclusive, represents current understanding of its urban landscape in this period. The loss of the material fabric of medieval Swansea cannot be attributed solely to the 1941 Blitz and the subsequent re-development of the town centre (though these had the biggest impact on the town's historic street pattern): already in the nineteenth century, Swansea's industrial success and commercial expansion resulted in the replacement of older structures with newer buildings and removed much of its historic architecture, and also included canalization of the river Tawe along a new course. In Swansea today, the only surviving medieval buildings (indeed, the only pre-1800 buildings of any kind) are the ruins of the New Castle and the Hospital of St. David, now heavily restored and used as a public house.[31]

A small body of written records allows us to recover something of the vanished historic town of Swansea, particularly from the sixteenth century and later, but also in the form of charters and other documents dating from the twelfth century onwards. However, one piece of textual evidence stands out for the particularly rich insights it can offer into

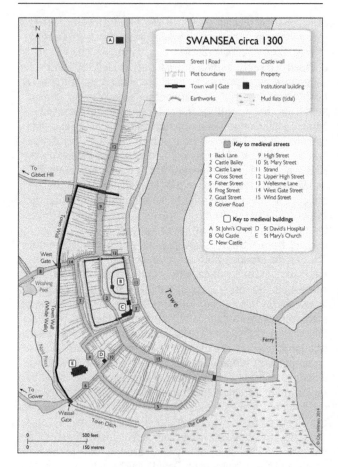

Figure 5. Swansea, ca. 1300.
© City Witness project, 2014.

the landscape and lives of the medieval town. The records of the canonization proceedings for Thomas Cantilupe, Bishop of Hereford, gathered in MS Vat. Lat. 4015, include nine witness statements attesting to events surrounding the hanging of the Welshman William Cragh by William de Briouze, the Anglo-Norman marcher lord of Gower, in Swansea in 1290. Cragh's revival after the hanging was attributed as a miracle to Thomas Cantilupe and in 1307, papal commissioners were sent to interview the witnesses, at inquests conducted in London and Hereford. The nine witness statements reflect a wide range of social, ethnic and cultural perspectives (albeit mediated by the Latin prose of the papal notaries), including lord, burgess and outlaw; religious and lay; male and female; Anglo-Norman and Welsh.

The William Cragh material in MS Vat. Lat. 4015 has been investigated in detail by a number of scholars including, most notably, Robert Bartlett in his detailed and perceptive micro-history *The Hanged Man*.[32] Bartlett uses the case of Cragh's execution and supposedly miraculous revival as a window into cultural perspectives, religious beliefs, and politics in the medieval marcher lordship of Gower. Yet there is a striking absence in Bartlett's book. It contains no map of medieval Swansea, nor any images of the medieval town itself (the only medieval site photographed is Oystermouth Castle, which was attacked by Cragh, a few miles away from Swansea in the village of Mumbles). The invisibility of medieval Swansea in Bartlett's book is unsurprising and understandable, given the difficulties of recovering the geography and material fabric of the pre-modern town. Bartlett does discuss the ways in which the nine witnesses conceptualize and articulate space and distances, calling attention to their use of subjective, embodied perspectives and formulae measured by their own experiences and actions (pp. 53–67). Yet the Cragh text presents a rare opportunity to examine the experiences, itineraries, and perceptions of the medieval witnesses within a very specific, spatially-situated context. In particular, it is rare to be able to reconstruct and analyze in detail the itineraries of such a socially-diverse range of individuals within the same geographical space. This, then, was the goal of the "City Witness" project: to link a new edition of the nine witness statements relating to the hanging of William Cragh with a new map of medieval Swansea ca. 1300, allowing the research team to reconstruct the speakers' reported positions and routes, and to explore their perspectives—both literal and figurative—within the town. This process of analysis and mapping reveals what Paul Strohm, drawing on the work of Michel de Certeau and Pierre Bourdieu, has called the "meaning-making activities" associated with medieval spaces.[33] The nine witness statements reflect the ways in which individuals shape, negotiate, and interpret the medieval urban landscape of Swansea, as well as the ways in which their own behaviour, in turn, is prescribed through the distinctive meanings attached to particular spaces.[34] In the witnesses' accounts, the importance of the town's invisible geographies emerges: the presence of unseen borders, boundaries, thresholds, and barriers, as well as the distinctive associations attached by particular social groups to specific sites. These invisible landscapes are constituted by social and cultural practices—regulations, pressures, memories, and traditions—which often exert a more powerful influence on Swansea's inhabitants than the physical, material geographies of the medieval town.

Some of the social and political realities of medieval Swansea were, of course, written very visibly and legibly on the material environment of the town. The gallows on Swansea's Gibbet Hill—the place of Cragh's execution—inevitably feature prominently in the medieval witness statements. It is clear, also, that the gallows were visible throughout the town and its environs, staging the power and authority of the Anglo-Norman marcher lord within the landscape. The priest Thomas Marshall is one of the witnesses who mentions the elevated location of the gallows, describing their position as

> [...] in quodam monte prope villam predictam, et possunt uideri dicte furce a castro et a villa, et distant a castro circa duos tractus baliste.

> [...] on a certain mound near the aforesaid town, and the said gallows can be seen from the castle and from the town, and is about two crossbow shots away from the castle.[35]

Other witnesses also use the formulation of "two crossbow shots" to express the distance of the gallows from the castle (for example, Adam of Loughor, fols. 226r–v); the lord's steward, John of Baggeham, prefers the formula "quasi per quartam partem unius miliaris a dicto castro" ("about a quarter of one Roman mile distant from the said castle"), and William de Briouze junior, son of the Lord William who ordered the hanging, recalls it as "circa mediam leucam Anglicanam" ("around half an English league") from the castle (fol. 223v, fol. 10r–v; for detailed analysis of the location of the gallows, see Further Reading). Strikingly, the majority of the witnesses have a clear view of the gallows and Cragh's execution, wherever they are in the town. Henry Skinner, a local man of property, probably connected with Swansea's thriving leather trade, watches from the foot of the gallows, where he sees the crossbeam break and Cragh and Trahaearn ap Hywel, the other condemned man, fall to the ground. He is also close enough to witness the bodily signs of death in Cragh (fol. 225v). Yet the hanging can also seen by others across the streets and environs of the medieval town, including the Welshman John ap Hywel, who watches with a crowd near St. Mary's Church (fol. 227r), and William de Briouze junior, who views events together with his household ("familia") from the window of the castle's first-floor hall ("de aula dicti castri," fol. 10v). Even in the case of the gallows, however, the town's visible landscape is inhabited by other, unseen, cultural geographies. The location of the gallows on a hill, outside the town, inevitably recalls the biblical site of Calvary or Golgotha, outside Jerusalem, where Christ was crucified, suggesting a range of *passio* or hagiographic tropes which colour the statements of some of the witnesses and influence the ways in which they interpret events. Lady Mary de Briouze, for example, is alone in insisting that Cragh's body made a "painful" journey back from Gibbet Hill on a wooden wheel, recalling the tortures and punishments of hagiographic tradition (fol. 8r), while William of Codineston, the chaplain, describes Cragh's weeping and penitence on his way to the gallows (fol. 13r).

Other material markers within the medieval landscape of Swansea also helped to shape the experiences and identities of those within the town, including the walls to the north and west of the town, as well as defensive ditches to the south and around the Castle Bailey enclosure; the gates into the Anglo-Norman town; and the New Castle, rising above the rest of the urban landscape and overlooking the busy harbour on the River Tawe from its sharp promontory. Features of natural topography, including the steep hills around the town, the marshy areas to the south and west, and the Tawe itself—an important locus for trade and communication—also helped to condition the spatial practices of inhabitants. Yet many configurations of space and social practice within medieval towns relied on invisible divisions and bounds, understood and negotiated habitually by inhabitants and visitors. Such unseen geographies operate in parish boundaries, bounds of liberties and rights and, in the of the broader geographical context of Swansea, the complex and overlapping territorial formulations of town, marcher lordship (Gower), diocese (St. David's), and historic Welsh kingdom (Deheubarth). We glimpse these imbricated geographies—though in a neat formula which elides the tensions between them—in Lady Mary de Briouze's description of her town as

> Sweyneseye, in terra de Gouer, Menevensis dyocesis, que terra erat de iurisdictione temporali dicti domini Willelmi, viri sui quondam [...]

> Swansea, in the region of Gower, in the diocese of St. David's, and the region was in the temporal jurisdiction of the said William, formerly her husband [...] (fol. 8r)

The itineraries reported by the nine witnesses in the William Cragh case reveal further aspects of the invisible urban landscape of medieval Swansea, and the ways in which different individuals and communities within the town are alert to, and affected by, varying social and cultural geographies.

The hanged man himself, William Cragh, recounts how he is held in the dungeon of the New Castle on the night before his execution, where he receives a vision of the Virgin Mary and Thomas Cantilupe. On the morning of the hanging, he is led out of the Castle Bailey, along West Gate Street and out through the town's West Gate, probably then following the path alongside the Washing Lake Brook, until it meets Gallows Road, where it climbs steeply up the hill. In this part of his journey, Cragh is made to participate in the public staging of the Anglo-Norman lord's power within the landscape of Swansea and its environs: by leaving the walled town, he is symbolically expelled from the local community and executed in the highly visible location of Gibbet Hill. But Cragh's itinerary after his body leaves the gallows opens up a range of more subtle and suggestive aspects of the town's cultural landscape. After being taken down from the gibbet, Cragh's lifeless body is carried to the Chapel of St. John (also referred to in medieval sources as St. John iuxta Swansea). Not all the witnesses mention the Chapel, yet those who do so evidently recognize its significance in the narrative. While the Chapel is locked, and Cragh's body cannot be laid inside as his friends hoped, it is clearly worthy of note that they try to carry him there. The Chapel of St. John had a particular association with Swansea's Welsh community in the Middle Ages, and a history which may well have reached back before Norman colonization. The Chapel was known as "Eglwys Ieuan" in Welsh, with the term *eglwys* recognized as a good indicator of early (pre-Norman) ecclesiastical sites.[36] Edith Evans comments that "there are good reasons why this cannot be the case" for the Chapel of St. John, as it is known to have been founded by the Knights Hospitaller in the mid-twelfth century.[37] Yet it is of course possible that this was a re-foundation on an earlier ecclesiastical site. Archaeological and mapping work has identified a large elliptical enclosure at the northern end of the medieval town, which the medieval Chapel of St. John was within. Early elliptical enclosures have been identified across the Gower landscape, where Jonathan Kissock suggests they may represent early "agricultural estates, perhaps associated with the church or even preserving earlier Roman land holdings."[38] The enclosure around St. John's could also be suggestive of an early Celtic monastic site, inside a "curvilinear" wall or ditch, typically located in "lower-lying ground or lower valley slopes" in a "coastal situation" (but not immediately on the coast itself).[39] The site could be identified, then, as a pre-Norman settlement nucleus, pre-dating the colonial marcher town. In 1290, the Chapel of St. John was outside the town walls of Swansea, on the Upper High Street where it led north through a growing suburb towards the Carmarthen road. This extra-mural location would itself have been a significant factor for those carrying Cragh's body: while the agents of Lord William de Briouze would undoubtedly have been keen to avoid taking the body back through Swansea's central streets (and perhaps creating a dangerous disturbance), Cragh's Welsh family and friends may have also preferred a resting-place outside the greater regulation and scrutiny of the walled Anglo-Norman town. The association between the Chapel and the Knights Hospitaller may also not have been unimportant for Cragh and his companions: the order had another foundation at Llanrhidian in Gower, the parish from which Cragh came (referenced in Cragh's witness deposition, fol. 220r).

The complex history, associations, and likely mythology of the Chapel of St. John for medieval inhabitants of Swansea and Gower calls attention, once again, to the invisible geographies which operated within the medieval town and which shaped the spatial imaginaries and behaviours of those who inhabited or frequented it. The archaeological, historical, and topographical evidence here help to explain the decision to bring Cragh's body to this particular location, reflecting collective memories, spatial practices, and traditions distinctive to the Welsh community in medieval Swansea. These kinds of nuances and associations can be elided by the initial appearance of a medieval town such as Swansea, with its single parish church of St. Mary's. Llinos Smith comments that "the majority of Welsh urban centres were single-parish communities, a true *corpus Christianum* where church and urban community were conjoined."[40] Yet the attitudes of the medieval Swansea witnesses to the Chapel of St. John, together with what we can recover of its history and significance to the local community, suggest that this image of a united urban body sharing a single place of worship and religious identification may be simplistic. In Swansea, the Church of St. Mary, a twelfth-century foundation, seems to have been associated much more strongly with the Anglo-Norman town and its marcher lords. In the event, William Cragh's friends find the Chapel of St. John locked—perhaps a suggestion that the Knights Hospitaller were keen to avoid implication in the tense events surrounding the Rhys ap Maredudd rebellion (1287) and Cragh's execution—and Cragh is instead taken to the nearby house of a burgess, Thomas Mathews. Cragh's itinerary reminds us of the complex, nuanced meanings invested in spaces within the urban landscape, as well as the presence of multiple boundaries and thresholds which score through the urban environment. Whether visible and material or invisible and "virtual," these boundaries reflect the intersection and competition of "crisscrossing jurisdictions" within the medieval town,[41] and the ways in which members of different cultural and ethnic communities engage with varying, unseen urban geographies.

It would be simplistic, however, to regard these differences in the understanding and use of Swansea's urban landscape purely in terms of an ethnic duality between Anglo-Norman and Welsh. The collection of witness statements in the William Cragh case indicates the presence of a range of invisible boundaries and barriers which operate according to ethnicity, but also gender, class, and other aspects of social status. Lady Mary de Briouze remains in her chamber in the New Castle throughout the events surrounding Cragh's execution, reflecting spatial constraints relating to gender as well as her noble status. While her prayers for intercession from Thomas Cantilupe are instrumental in the miraculous recovery of Cragh, her actions are limited to the domestic sphere of her chamber, and group of female attendants, within the castle (fols. 8r–9r). Mary's knowledge of the

wider events in her town is constituted purely by "vox communis et communis oppinio gencium et fama publica" ("the
voice of the community and common opinion of the people
and public rumour," fol. 10r): for her, the geography of much
of Swansea is assembled out of the words of messengers
and second-hand reports. The movements of Lady Mary's
stepson, William de Briouze junior, also seem to be restricted
by his noble status and, probably, his association with the
unpopular (or, at least, divisive) marcher administration. He
too remains in the castle during the hanging itself, albeit with
his clear view towards the gallows from a window, only later
venturing to see the recovering Cragh in the house of Thomas
Mathews (fols. 10r–13r). The de Briouze family chaplain, William of Codineston, casts light on further thresholds and
barriers which operate invisibly within the urban landscape.
Codineston accompanies the execution squad, together with
Cragh and Trahaearn ap Hywel, probably as far as the town's
West Gate. He describes Cragh's display of weeping and penitence here, significantly located within the walled space of
the town and legible as a sign of contrition towards the community which he has, through his outlawry and attack on the
castle at Oystermouth, wronged. But Codineston explains
that he is unable to accompany Cragh as he is led out of the
walled town: the subsequent part of his witness statement is
based, like Lady Mary's, on the reports of others. Codineston
states explicitly that he was unable to go in person to Gibbet
Hill due to his status as a priest:

> [...] sed dictus testis non fuerat presens, ut
> dixit, quando dicta oratione facta fuit, quia
> propter officium sacerdotale noluit sequi dictos
> malefactores quando ad suspendium duceban-
> tur extra villam de Sweyneseye.

> [...] but the said witness was not present in
> person, as he said, when the said speech was
> made, because of his priestly office he did not
> wish to accompany the said criminals when
> they were led to be hanged outside of the town
> of Swansea. (fols. 13r–v)

It seems likely from Codineston's comments here that he did not want to associate himself with the shameful death of a criminal or the violence involved: he seems to have regarded the West Gate of Swansea as the point beyond which he should not pass, with his testimony noting specifically that the hanging was to take place "extra villam."

William of Codineston's testimony articulates perhaps most clearly the presence of invisible borders and boundaries within the medieval town. Although his journey stops at the West Gate, it is not the Gate itself which limits the chaplain's movement. Like the other material boundaries visible within the medieval urban landscape of Swansea, the walls and Gate are in fact porous and permeable, their power maintained more by social conventions and normative spatial practices—here Codineston's received notion of priestly decorum—than by any physical barrier. Carol Symes reminds us that, within medieval urban environments, individuals "would have been acutely aware that a network of virtual boundaries was being crossed and re-crossed. Sometimes these were invisible to certain people but obvious to others."42 In medieval Swansea, these unseen geographies—shaped by socially-constructed and accepted normative behaviours, by explicit regulation, and by distinctive traditions and memories—exert a far more compelling influence on the practices of inhabitants than the material features of the town's environment. The witnesses in the William Cragh case are each alert to different elements of Swansea's invisible townscape; they move, in general, within the same geographical space, but inhabit varying cultural and social landscapes. The rich material of MS Vat. Lat. 4015, then, helps us not only to reconstruct the material fabric of medieval Swansea, now lost from today's urban landscape, but also to recover the invisible realms experienced and negotiated by those within the medieval town.

Seeing the Absent Cityscape:
Regeneration and Interpretation

The "City Witness" project in Swansea developed from an initial approach by Swansea Council, who were keen to confront
this challenge of linking the modern city to its medieval past.
In particular, the Council were keen to bridge the disconnec-
tion between the surviving ruins of the castle in the city centre and the surrounding urban environment: shops and residential accommodation on the High Street, the paved area
(created in the 1990s) at Castle Square, office blocks, and the
1970s Quadrant Shopping Centre nearby. The Council's aspirations were driven by pressing economic imperatives. The
city centre or High Street area of Swansea was targeted for
regeneration and had received significant EU Convergence
funding (directed at regions where GDP per capita is below 75
percent of the European Union average). The Council aimed
to develop Swansea city centre as its "Castle Quarter," with a
distinctive identity grounded in heritage, as well as attractive
tourism and retail offers. The "City Witness" project was conceived as a response to Swansea Council's request, and as
an experiment in using new research to drive both heritage
interpretation and economic development. As well as the
AHRC funding, Swansea Council contributed match funding
towards a series of seventeen cast iron pavement markers
throughout the city centre, marking the location of key sites
and features within the medieval town. These were linked
to a traditional tour leaflet, as well as an interactive digital tour map with multi-media interpretation resources and
visualizations of locations within the medieval town. These
visualizations were key to the project strategy of engaging
local people and visitors with Swansea's now absent, invisible
past, and provided an opportunity to experiment with different ways of picturing the town in the Middle Ages. The pavement marker project and visualizations of Swansea's medieval townscape both foreground, once again, questions about
the invisible city and the implications of attempting to see an
absent historic landscape, both for the wider non-academic
community and for specialist researchers.

Visualizing historic landscapes is, of course, an area fraught with controversy and conflicting methodological and ideological approaches. While digital technologies for modelling and visualizing historic environments present huge opportunities for public engagement (particularly at sites where material survival is limited), as well as for exploring scholarly hypotheses, debate continues about the most appropriate modes and principles for pursuing such visual recreations. A variety of initiatives and documents have attempted to prescribe models of best practice in the digital visualization of historic landscapes, including the *London Charter for the Computer-based Visualisation of Cultural Heritage* (http://www.londoncharter. org/, 2009), and the 2012 report produced by the "Visualisation in Archaeology" project, a partnership between the UK Archaeology Data Service and English Heritage, which sought to "contribute towards the construction of an intellectual framework for the visualization of archaeological data based on applied research" (see Further Reading). Documents such as these reflect concerns with the representation of uncertainty or conjecture, strategies for making explicit links to the underpinning data (or in some instances the lack of it), and the difficult balance between creative re-imagination and conservative adherence to (what may be limited or incomplete) evidence bases. While new technologies have pushed the question of visualization to the forefront of critical agendas in archaeology and landscape history, the broad questions raised by debates such as these take us back to recurrent conversations about the relationship between imagination and empirical research in geography and historical studies more widely. Already in 1947, the geographer John Wright was able to explore "the place of the imagination in geography," acknowledging that "a powerful imagination is a dangerous tool in geography unless it be used with care," and that creative or subjective approaches are often, sometimes rightly, "held in disrepute" by scholars.[43] Yet Wright also considers the ways in which scholarly imagination "projects itself into *terrae incognitae* and suggests routes for us to follow, but also plays upon those things that we discover and out of them makes imaginative conceptions which we seek to share with others," concluding that he does "not regard the scientific and the aesthetic either as mutually exclusive or as antagonistic in geography" (p. 10).

The *terrae incognitae* of Swansea's lost medieval landscape invite creative and imaginative engagement as much as diligent empirical research. The process of visualizing medieval Swansea provided an opportunity to test out varied theories about the urban landscape of the town in the Middle Ages, in different visual idioms and artistic styles, from watercolour to digital renders. The visualizations also allowed us to hypothesize and examine the sight-lines and perspectives of our nine medieval witnesses, analyzing the impact of the topography and built features of the town in the events surrounding William Cragh's execution. The outcome of this visualization process was a variety of different representations of the medieval town, embracing the notion of different ways of witnessing the same space and deliberately foregrounding multivocality in interpretation.[44] The visualizations permitted a particular kind of imaginative inquiry (while still based where possible on the mapping evidence), immersive and experiential critical engagement, and creative experiment, which helped to develop new insights into the spaces of medieval Swansea and how they were used. But seeing the invisible city only takes us so far. Some recent commentators have warned of the limitations of visualizations as a tool for critical engagement and interpretation. The landscape archaeologist Vincent Gaffney, for example, has challenged the primacy attached to seeing, as a proxy for understanding, in modern western society, highlighting the "emphasis on or (perhaps) the fetishization of visual experience" in contemporary culture and the ubiquitous equation of sight with knowledge across a range of cultural contexts.[45] Moving beyond the visualizations themselves, the "City Witness" project also developed a game based on the mapping data for medieval Swansea and the witness statements in MS Vat. Lat. 4015. Players are invited to navigate the medieval townscape, interview witnesses, collect evidence, and

Figure 6. What did you see? Game, website screenshot
(www.medievalswansea.ac.uk). © City Witness project, 2014.

reach their own conclusions about what really happened in the strange case of William Cragh, casting their own vote in a tally collected online in real time. The game represents an attempt to move beyond the merely visual as a mode of knowledge, encouraging participants to use (even if in limited ways) empathy, affect, critical agency, problem-solving skills, intuition, and imagination to enable their engagement with Swansea's medieval past.

Lost and Dreamed Cityscapes

The need for such creative leaps and imaginative commitment is of course particularly great in Swansea, where so little of the medieval town—indeed, as we have seen, so little even of the pre-war town so beloved of Dylan Thomas—survives. The single most transformative event for the historic landscape of Swansea was certainly the "Three Nights' Blitz" of February 1941, which caused the widespread devastation, and eventually the radical re-planning, of the town centre.[46] The 1941 Blitz subjected Swansea to three nights of attack from both explosive and incendiary bombs. Surprisingly, German operational documents show that the heavy destruction inflicted on the town centre was no accident: rather than targeting the docks or industrial sites, these particular raids were directed at commercial and residential areas in an apparent attempt to undermine local morale (Alban, p. 132). The Swansea Blitz had a tragic human cost, leaving 203 people killed, 409 injured, and over seven thousand people homeless. It also left forty-one acres (about seventeen hectares) of the town centre in ruins (Alban, pp. 131–2). A local eyewitness, quoted in the local newspaper the *South Wales Evening Post* on Monday, February 24, 1941, describes the scene during the air raids:

> Tumultuous seas of fire and great smoke clouds which threw back a red glow and accompanied by a terrific roar of flame was the last impression I had of the town after being driven from my post of fire-watcher in Swansea on Friday night. (p. 3)

Excerpts from the official report on the "Three Nights' Blitz," presented by the local Air Raid Precautions Controller to the local Council in March 1941, give further evidence of the scale of the destruction to the historic fabric of Swansea's town centre. The Controller outlines some of the key features of the damage found by investigators on the morning of Saturday 22 February.

> What did we find on that Saturday morning? Roads damaged and impassable. Sewers damaged. Electric cables and equipment damaged. 15 Schools destroyed or seriously damaged. [...]
>
> The Town's Shopping Centre wiped out, including the Market. Shops rendered useless by being destroyed by bombs or being burned out, or by having delayed action bombs in front of them.
>
> 171 Food Shops gone—64 Grocers, 61 Butchers, 12 Bakers and 34 Hotels Restaurants and Cafes gone. This figure does not deal with the Green Grocers and other Stalls in the lost market, but to illustrate to you from the Market point of view, there were 43 Butchers' Holdings in the Market and those 43 Butchers supplying no less than 22,000 customers. [...]
>
> St. Mary's church and other places of Worship destroyed.[47]

The Air Raid Precautions Controller focuses, understandably, on the damage to Swansea's infrastructure and its social and commercial amenities. But the area of most severe devastation also corresponded with the historic centre of the town.

In a study of bomb ruins in twentieth-century British fiction, Leo Mellor has written on the "amnesia-inducing hidden strata" of the devastated city; the "haunted" landscape left by wartime destruction.[48] In *Return Journey*, of course, the "havoc'd" streets of Swansea are a prompt to memory, both collective and personal, as Thomas wills the lost town into being through words and seeks the vanished "Young

Thomas" who represents his own youth and that of his generation. But Thomas's attempts to recover the past through Swansea's changed, ravaged landscape ultimately fails: the radio play ends with the repeated word "Dead" (p. 118); the youthful Thomas and his town have disappeared. Mellor, in fact, acknowledges the ambivalence and complexity of bomb sites as loci of both remembering and forgetting, describing their "absolute doubleness" as signifiers of abruption and loss, and "a way of understanding a great swathe of linear time previously hidden or buried, offering history exposed to the air" (p. 6). In many towns and cities, bomb damage offered the opportunity and impetus for the archaeological investigation of urban sites in the 1940s and 1950s.[49] In Swansea, however, the priority was to return the devastated town to a functioning commercial centre with appropriate amenities and infrastructure for its inhabitants in the post-war years, and into the future.

Here another set of intriguing invisible geographies enters Swansea's history: the unbuilt, dreamed post-war cityscapes, proposed by planners but never constructed. The first plans for the re-development of Swansea town centre began in 1942, with the Borough Engineer, J.R. Heath, presenting the draft *County Borough of Swansea Draft Scheme for Re-Planning and Re-Development of the Central Town Area: Plan and Explanatory Notes* to the County Borough Council in 1943 (West Glamorgan Archives D 56/7/2). These initial, unrealized plans for Swansea included the construction of a processional way, linking the town centre with the Guildhall: in effect a kind of fantasy "re-medievalizing" of the city, with a view to urban ceremony and pageantry. This scheme, however, was dismissed as it required the purchase and demolition of many properties which had escaped bomb damage. Heath's 1943 scheme represents a complete, holistic, re-design of Swansea town centre, with specific zones or "areas" envisaged for functions such as shopping, "places of amusement," and "hotels" (sections 10 and 12). The scheme proposes an ambitious "Foreshore Development Area" along the seafront towards Mumbles, but acknowledges that this would require the removal or re-location of numerous transport and industrial sites (section 15). The Catalogue of Objections from local residents, freeholders, and business-holders to the various re-development plans (and the Compulsory Purchase Orders entailed within them) includes complaints largely on the grounds (sometimes demonstrably incorrect) that premises had not received significant bomb damage, though they also reflect a mixed attitude to Swansea's built heritage (West Glamorgan Archives (52/55). While Objection 158 argues against the demolition of Lewis Lewis's Store on the High Street, on the grounds that the building is a rare pre-1850 survival, the Council's response to Objection 268 (removal of the Bush Hotel, High Street), notes that "[p]roperty in this street is generally 70 to 100 years old and ripe for redevelopment." The first Compulsory Purchase Orders, under the terms of the Town and Country Planning Act, 1944, were made from 1946 onwards. The re-development scheme eventually implemented included new roads and traffic management systems, beginning with the opening of the Kingsway—a new, modern-style thoroughfare designed for cars—in 1950, and the construction of new buildings throughout the town centre during the following decade. The re-built St. Mary's Church opened in 1959, and a new covered market in 1961. Finally, the town's Quadrant Shopping Centre opened in the late 1970s, as the city began to turn its attention to regeneration of its former dockland and maritime areas. The imagined, alternative versions of Swansea which haunt today's urban landscape are far from unique: many other cities in both the pre- and post-war period experimented with ambitious re-development plans which were never implemented (see Further Reading). The new plan eventually selected for Swansea, however, did have a radical impact in erasing much of the town's historic street pattern and the links between the modern urban landscape and its medieval past. As we have seen, excepting the ruins of Swansea Castle and the much-restored St. David's Hospital, the town of the Middle Ages is now no longer legible in the modern cityscape; bombed, re-built, and scoured of its visible medieval fabric.

After these radical ruptures and dislocations to Swansea's historic townscape, the "City Witness" pavement marker scheme took on an ambitious challenge: to reinstate Swansea's medieval urban landscape within the modern city; to make the invisible visible. But the actual experience of walking the marker trail provoked responses—and critical implications—which the research team had not foreseen. The pavement markers were installed at seventeen locations, including the gates of the medieval town, the town walls, the medieval marketplace on Wind Street, the site of St. John's Chapel (now the nineteenth-century building of St. Matthew's Church), and the Strand, where the enduring street name is the only reminder of its former character as a busy waterfront area. An interactive online map linked to the pavement markers includes multi-media resources such as images, text, and information about artefacts found at each location, as well as GPS data, meaning that users can encounter medieval Swansea in the streets of the modern city, via their phones or other mobile devices. Users can toggle between layers on the digital map, allowing them to navigate by the medieval townscape of Swansea or by its modern lay-out, or by overlaying the two to explore contrasts and differences. And, as shown by the screenshot in Figure 7, this is often quite a disorienting, unsettling experience. Today, in Swansea, you can walk through walls, slipping through the invisible ghosts of the former medieval fortifications. You can cross a busy dual carriageway where the city's South Gate and Cadle Stream would have been, walking over solid ground where once you would have sunk into tidal marsh and mud flats. You can stand on what would have been the shore of a great river and the heart of a busy harbour, where now there's a retail park and industrial estate. Modern and medieval geographies pull against each other. There's a strong, even violent, sense of disjunction and rupture from the city's past. Early test users of the pavement marker trail in Swansea commented emphatically on this vertiginous—yet arresting—sense of tension between the medieval and modern cityscape.

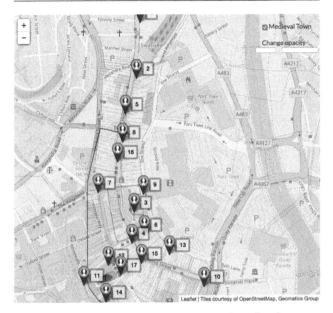

Figure 7. Layered map of modern and medieval
Swansea, website screenshot
(www.medievalswansea.ac.uk).
© City Witness project, 2014.

And yet, much heritage discourse—particularly in the applied
context of interpretation for public audiences—is predicated
on neat notions of smooth continuity and contiguity. Extant
historic fabric, or "surviving physical relics," are a privileged
primary resource, particularly in urban contexts, for interpretation and commodification as heritage,[50] with visually-recog-
nizable historic character a defining element for a landscape
receptive to heritage tourism.[51] Interpretation resources in
historic locations commonly invite visitors to "step into history," relying on material survivals (or sometimes restorations
and reconstructions) as a visible conduit into the past. The
accessibility of history is measured by its visible presence in

the landscape: the singular power of these material "relics" to engage and transport viewers is assumed as a given, and rarely scrutinized. Continuity in the urban environment, and the survival of built heritage, helps to foster a sense of direct, immediate connection with history, supporting a linear narrative which links past and present to engage public imagination.[52] Yet the language of linear connection, continuity and proximity served to the public in much urban heritage interpretation contrasts markedly with current scholarly and theoretical work on the city, especially that emerging from critical geography and cultural studies. While conventional heritage interpretation resources formulate a narrative of linear connection located in a privileged environment of material continuity, theoretical approaches to space and time in the city envisage a much more dynamic, complex, problematic relationship between locations, individuals, and historical moments. Mike Crang, for example, has written of "the polychronic city as a realm of shattered and fragmented times;" a "folded or haunted" space in which multiple histories overlay and converge.[53] Elsewhere, Crang, collaborating with Penny Travlou, foregrounds "friction" between the visible fabric of a city and its invisible, remembered pasts, viewing the relationship between space and time as one of "uncomfortable provocations" rather than in terms of stable conduits into a neatly-ordered history.[54]

The problematic divergence between the applied discourse of heritage interpretation and theoretical discussion of the city places pressure on the public dissemination of new research into urban history and historic environments, such as that produced by the "City Witness" project. Converting the language of academic research into the conventional discourse of heritage interpretation—with its pervasive model of continuity and linear connection—threatens a further process of commodification and simplification, with complex scholarly ideas about urban space and time stripped away for export to a public audience. But, in Swansea, the conventional heritage model of visual recognition and accessibility, of engaging with the past through its visible material survivals, clearly cannot operate. The notion of linear continuity or connection, with the past visibly proximate to the present, fails to articulate the feeling of dislocation when the historic landscape collides with a radically different modern environment. This almost visceral sense of dislocation and estrangement—experienced, for example, when walking across the course of an absent river or passing through the line of a lost fortification—is itself a powerful tool for imaginative engagement with the past, its energy generated by physical abruptions and contrasts rather than material continuities. As an alternative approach to engaging the public with urban heritage, such an emphasis on tensions, frictions, and dislocations within the urban landscape opens up possibilities beyond those determined by accidents of survival in the built environment. It invites local communities and visitors to think in more dynamic ways about the relationships between past and present, moving beyond the stylized, usually fallacious model of linear continuity and connection. Crucially, this approach also allows current research (and the theoretical positions which inform it) to be shared with integrity rather than being re-packaged and fundamentally altered for wider public dissemination. The Swansea pavement markers map engages users with the complexity of the city's history and changing landscape, foregrounding the radical transformations and ruptures which have formed its environment and catalyzing reflection on changing cultures, pressures and priorities in the local area. The layered map, with its "copresent, different times" (Crang and Travlou, p. 169), brings the pluralities and tensions of the city into focus, and invites users to see Swansea in arresting new ways, re-making familiar places and their meanings and producing a distinctive heritage landscape with absence and invisibility at its imaginative centre.

A Place and its Lives: Wassail Square

In the final section of this chapter, I want to present a short case study of one location in the cityscape of Swansea: its lives both visible and invisible, medieval and modern, and its presence within the "ghostly geography" (Crang and Trav-lou, p. 171) of the urban landscape. Through the example of Wassail Square, we can explore the ways in which multiple chronological and imaginative layers co-exist within the urban landscape, forming not a neat linear narrative, but rather a provocative, jostling cluster of spatial meanings and possibilities. On the map of medieval Swansea (Figure 5), Wassail Square can be found just outside the Wassail Gate, where the triangular or funnel-shaped formation marks the beginning of the road west to Gower. In the post-medieval period, Wassail Square (or "Wassail Street") was characterized by its inns and hostelries, probably developed in part due to its location on the western fringe of the town. In early guides to Swansea, the area also becomes known as "The World's End," again probably due to its association with lodgings for travellers at the edge of the town. The 1830 *Wales Illustrated in a Series of Views*, for example, notes that the area is "whimsically called 'The World's End' [...] where there are some excellent houses built for the accommodation of strangers," close to Mount Pleasant, a pleasure ground, and the esplanade.[55] Wassail Square endured heavy destruction during the Three Nights' Blitz of 1941, sustaining particularly heavy damage from incendiary bombs in the early hours of Saturday, February 22. Auxiliary Fire Service records log the "extensive" damage, including destruction of the Old Rutland Street School.[56] Wassail Square fell within the Compulsory Purchase Order zone of the 1947 re-development plans;[57] further house clearances in the 1960s led to its ultimate removal.[58] At this point, Wassail Square was permanently erased from the streetscape of Swansea.

Yet Wassail Square was already a strangely elusive location—in danger of slipping off the map and becoming invisible—in the Middle Ages. The location makes a curious appearance—or, more accurately, an intriguing absence—in the records of MS Vat. Lat. 4015, in the witness testimony of John ap Hywel, a local Welsh labourer who gives his account of events to the papal commissioners in Hereford. John tells us that he watches the hanging of William Cragh from an open area near the Church of St. Mary. The deposition records: "ipse testis existens cum centum personis ut estimat in platea ville de Swayneseie prope ecclesiam Sancte Marie" ("the witness himself was with one hundred people (in his estimate) in the square in the town of Swansea near the church of St. Mary," fol. 227r). *Platea* would suggest an open square or wide street, but probably not a churchyard, which would probably have been denoted more explicitly.[59] Michael Richter assumes that this location was within the town walls of Swansea ("innerhalb der Stadtmauer"),[60] but John ap Hywel does not state this explicitly, and it is difficult to identify an appropriate location in this area, which could have accommodated one hundred spectators, other than the churchyard of St. Mary's. A location immediately inside the Wassail Gate or adjacent to St. Mary's Church would also have had its sightlines significantly limited by the proximity of the town walls, making John's ability to witness the hanging directly, as he claims, more doubtful. Instead, it is more likely that John, and the rest of the crowd, watched the hanging from the triangular or funnel-shaped area just outside the Wassail Gate— Wassail Square—where they would have had a clear view up along the western edge of the town towards Gibbet Hill. It is possible, in fact, that this area may have functioned as a secondary market place for the medieval town, supplementing the main Anglo-Norman market adjacent to the castle at the top of Wind Street, with its location just outside the walls suggesting that it may have primarily served the local Welsh community. Triangular or funnel-shaped forms have been identified as characteristic of earlier medieval marketplaces, before the introduction of planned market squares in the later Middle Ages.[61] These forms are particularly associated with monastic towns, where they are found outside abbey walls and gateways.[62] A similar spatial configuration could well have led to the organic development of a market place outside Wassail Gate in medieval Swansea: an obvious place for commercial activity, at a busy thoroughfare and landmark, just outside the formal controls of the town itself. On the road west, leading to the Gower peninsula, the site would have been particularly convenient and attractive for the local Welsh community, and gathering or trading here may have been as much a positive choice as the result of any exclusion or disenfranchisement in Swansea's main urban market.

Once again, the testimony of John ap Hywel reminds us of the invisible social and cultural geographies operating within the medieval town, which slip easily past the perception of those who are not alert to them. The papal notaries, recording John's testimony in 1307, are not attuned to the significance of specific spaces within Swansea or their association with particular social, cultural and economic practices. Their use of the highly generalized term *platea* obscures the specificity of John's location and elides the complex set of pressures, traditions, and personal choices which together determine his location on the day of the hanging. Similarly, Michael Richter's assumption that the *platea* was inside the town walls of Swansea misses the nuances of spatial practice here, and the presence of unseen cultural divisions and distinctions within the medieval urban landscape. The three-dimensional digital visualizations produced by the "City Witness" project allow us to view Swansea's medieval environment from the inside, testing hypotheses about sight-lines and witnesses' perspectives. But, more importantly, these digital models also encourage us to think about the invisible landscape of Swansea: the hidden constraints, norms, or pressures which constitute the real barriers and thresholds within the medieval town and condition the spatial practices of individuals.

Today, the historic Wassail Square has vanished; its name is no longer on any street maps of Swansea. And yet, it *does* still exist in a re-imagined form—in the central area of the city's 1970s Quadrant Shopping Centre. This central covered court, featuring the Debenhams department store, a coffee shop, and public benches, is called Wassail Square, with the arcades leading to it named after other lost streets from the pre-war town.[63] While official plans of the shopping mall show the names, they are no longer used by local people: "Wassail Square" now functions primarily as the postal address for businesses in the inner zone of the Quadrant Centre.[64]

The site of the Wassail Gate itself is now shown by one of the "City Witness" pavement markers, just outside the Quadrant Centre doors where they open onto Whitewalls Street (another name inhabited by the ghost of Swansea's medieval townscape).

Finally, an article by the Swansea historian Gerald Gabb has presented a provocative re-evaluation of post-war urban planning in Swansea (often the subject of criticism and denigration) and has asked us to imagine "that Goering had directed the mass raids of Junkers, Heinkels and Dorniers somewhere else."[65] With the historic centre spared the devastation of the Blitz, Gabb draws a map of a very different twenty-first-century Swansea, in which much historic architecture, as well as the medieval street-plan, has survived, though old buildings are increasingly dilapidated and the town is intersected with concrete flyovers and new traffic management systems (p. 26; Gabb uses the "older streets" and "flyovers" of the neighbouring town of Port Talbot, which avoided major bombing, as a comparator). Gabb describes a "forest of tower blocks" in the High Street area, and finally turns his imagination to Wassail Square and its environs:

> The housing between the market and the gasworks is now the least desirable in town— Wassail Square is the worst—and there have been several plans over the last twenty years to sweep it away. Nothing has yet been done [...] (p. 26)

Gabb's counterfactual or alternative history of post-war Swansea interposes a further version of the invisible city within today's urban landscape: an imagined, parallel Swansea which offers a counterpoint to the actual decisions of planners and re-developers since 1945. In this alternative Swansea, the medieval townscape lingers, but undermined by neglect and the necessity of coping with increased car ownership. There is no sudden rupture, like that caused by the 1941 Blitz, but there is inevitably still change and compromise. What Gabb refers to as his "nightmare" vision of an unbombed Swansea (p. 26) brings another temporal haunting to Swansea's streets: a moment which never was, but which might have been.

In the case of Wassail Square, we see the complex, multiple layers to the cityscape of Swansea: distinctive, yet typical of any historic settlement. Past and present landscapes pull against each other, seen and unseen geographies operate both in conjunction and in tension, spaces gather unstable and dynamic meanings, and historical moments touch and collide in surprising, uncomfortable, and fertile ways. The many lives, visible and invisible, of Wassail Square include its medieval and post-medieval uses as a marketplace or centre for hospitality and festivity, as well as the precarious trace it leaves as an unnamed *platea* in the fourteenth-century testimony of a local Welsh labourer. It is a razed, blasted terrain after the 1941 Blitz, cleared away by developers in the push to re-build the post-war city. It persists, as the ghost of a place, in the modern setting of the shopping centre, largely unnoticed, and is now commodified as heritage in the "City Witness" pavement marker trail. It exists, also, in subjective perceptions and imagined versions, from the experiences shared by John ap Hywel and the others jostling in the crowd of spectators at Cragh's hanging, to the suggestive nineteenth-century notion of the "World's End" at the edge of the town, to Gabb's parallel, unbombed city centre, disintegrating into neglect and a different kind of slow, deliberate ruin.

The Swansea pavement marker project opens up questions about relationships between seeing and knowledge, between the lost historic landscape of Swansea and the present-day urban environment, and between visible and invisible geographies within the city. This chapter has explored the idea of seeing the invisible city in ways which bridge the Swansea of the Middle Ages and today, touching on a range of different kinds of invisible landscapes: social, cultural and subjective geographies which are never material and only ever visible to certain individuals and groups, as well as historic environments once physically present but now erased from the modern urban context. The challenge of seeing the

Figure 8. Example of pavement marker.
© City Witness project, 2014.

invisible city, of experimenting with ways of viewing unsee-able urban landscapes, thus brings together the scholarly analysis of medieval Swansea—the recovery of its lost mate-rial fabric, as well as exploration of the spatial practices of its inhabitants—and the interpretation and presentation of the absent medieval town for modern communities and vis-itors through the lens of heritage. But why does it matter to forge links between empirical research and heritage inter-pretation techniques, or between broad concepts across the medieval and modern city? What is at stake in this attempt to draw together historical scholarship, theories of the city and applied heritage practice, and to respond critically to their points of convergence and difference?

Reaching out beyond the academy with new research presents a vexed mixture of compromise and opportunity. Communicating with diverse audiences and partners can open up the possibility of more creative, risk-taking, and innovative methods, with potential benefits (both foreseen and unforeseen) for scholarship. But sharing scholarly research with wider publics can also result in complex ideas being re-packaged—sometimes simplified, with inherent complexities and uncertainties elided—for general consumption. In this instance, exporting the new work on medieval Swansea into the conventional discourse of heritage interpretation—with its emphasis on continuity and linear connection between past and present—risked a significant intellectual deficit, discarding current theoretical positions on the nature of urban time and space and mis-representing the intellectual context behind the research. While the layered digital map is not a fully satisfactory answer to this problem, it does catalyze users' engagement with dislocations, estrangements, and collisions within the urban landscape, dramatizing some of the issues explored by urban theorists and critical geographers such as Crang. Much as the urban environment includes multiple invisible geographies, the varied lenses of empirical medieval research, urban theory, and heritage interpretation offer contrasting ways of seeing them. Exploring the common ground shared by these approaches, as well as highlighting their frictions and disjunctions, offers fresh ways of viewing the invisible city in the medieval landscape and today, while acknowledging tensions between different modes of seeing, knowledge, and understanding.

Notes

[27] Dylan Thomas, *Return Journey*, in *Dylan Thomas Miscellany* (London: Dent, 1963), 101–18 at 101 and 108.

[28] Dylan Thomas, *Reminiscences of Childhood* (First Version), in *Dylan Thomas Miscellany*, 87–93 at 87.

[29] Edith Evans, *Swansea Castle and the Medieval Town* (Swansea: Glamorgan Gwent Archaeological Trust, 1983), 23; also see Further Reading.

[30] See http://www.qub.ac.uk/urban_mapping/index.htm.

[31] See Bernard Morris, "Buildings and Topography," in *The City of Swansea: Challenges and Change*, ed. Ralph A. Griffiths (Stroud: Sutton, 1990), 145–64 at 145.

[32] Robert Bartlett, *The Hanged Man: A Story of Miracle, Memory and Colonialism in the Middle Ages* (Princeton: Princeton University Press, 2006). For other work on the William Cragh text, see Further Reading.

[33] Paul Strohm, *Theory and the Premodern Text* (Minneapolis: University of Minnesota Press, 2000), 4.

[34] Barbara Hanawalt and Michael Kobialka observe that "Not only did people create uses for space, but having done so, that space could influence the behavior of those who occupied it, defining space tended to prescribe the behavior within it." See their introduction to *Medieval Practices of Space*, ed. Hanawalt and Kobialka (Minneapolis: University of Minnesota Press, 2000), ix–xviii, x.

[35] MS Vat. Lat. 4015, fol. 222v, ed. and trans. Harriett Webster (www.medievalswansea.ac.uk). All subsequent references to the William Cragh text will be taken from this edition.

[36] T. Roberts, "Welsh Ecclesiastical Place-Names and Archaeology," in *The Early Christian Church in Wales and the West*, ed. Nancy Edwards and Alan Lane (Oxford: Oxbow, 1992), 41–44 at 42.

[37] Edith Evans, *Early Medieval Ecclesiastical Sites in Southeast Wales*, GGAT report 2003/030 (Swansea: Glamorgan Gwent Archaeological Trust, 2003), 40.

[38] Keith Lilley and Gareth Dean, "Development of Medieval Swansea" (http://www.medievalswansea.ac.uk); Jonathan Kissock, "The Upland Dimension: Further Conjectures on Early Medieval Settlement in Gower," *Morgannwg* 35 (2001): 55–68.

[39] *An Inventory of the Ancient Monuments in Glamorgan: Pre-Norman*, Part 3, *The Early Christian Period* (Cardiff: Royal Commission on the Ancient and Historical Monuments of Wales, 1976), 12–13.

[40] Llinos B. Smith, "In Search of an Urban Identity: Aspects of Urban Society in Late Medieval Wales," in *Urban Culture in Medieval Wales*, ed. Helen Fulton (Cardiff: University of Wales Press, 2012), 19–50 at 30.

[41] Saskia Sassen, *Territory, Authority, Rights: From Medieval to Global Assemblages* (Princeton: Princeton University Press, 2006), 32.

[42] Carol Symes, "Out in the Open, in Arras: Sightlines, Soundscapes and the Shaping of a Medieval Public Sphere," in *Cities, Texts and Social Networks 400–1500: Experiences and Perceptions of Medieval Urban Space*, ed. Caroline Goodson, Anne E. Lester, and Carol Symes (Farnham: Ashgate, 2010), 279–302 at 294.

[43] John Wright, "Terrae Incognitae: The Place of the Imagination in Geography," *Annals of the Association of American Geographers* 37 (1947): 1–15 at 5.

[44] See http://www.medievalswansea.ac.uk/en/mapping/visualisations/.

[45] Vincent Gaffney, "In the Kingdom of the Blind: Visualization and E-Science in Archaeology, the Arts and Humanities," in *The Virtual Representation of the Past*, ed. Mark Greengrass and Lorna Hughes (Farnham: Ashgate, 2008), 125–34 at 127.

[46] Air raids on Swansea began from June 1940 (when German forces took possession of airfields in Brittany, bringing Swansea into range of the medium bomber planes), and included forty-four separate raids in total. But the "Three Nights' Blitz" caused by far the greatest damage. See J. R. Alban, "Picture Essay: The Second World War," in *The City of Swansea*, ed. Griffiths, 131–32.

[47] Official Report on the "Three Nights' Blitz" by Mr. Howell Lang Lang-Coath, Air Raid Precautions Controller for Swansea, to the Council of the County Borough of Swansea, 18 March 1941, West Glamorgan Archives (P/SM 95 (County Borough of Swansea, A.R.P. Miscellanea)), fols. 3–4.

[48] Leo Mellor, *Reading the Ruins: Modernism, Bombsites and British Culture* (Cambridge: Cambridge University Press, 2011), 165.

[49] C. Gerrard, *Medieval Archaeology: Understanding Traditions and Contemporary Approaches* (London: Routledge, 2003), 88–89.

[50] G. J. Ashworth, "From History to Heritage: From Heritage to Identity: In Search of Concepts and Models," in *Building a New Heritage: Tourism, Culture and Identity in the New Europe*, ed. G. J. Ashworth and P. J. Larkham (London: Routledge, 1994), 13–30 at 16.

[51] John Urry and Jonas Larsen, *The Tourist Gaze 3.0* (London: Sage, 2011), 4.

[52] For a discussion of the power of linear narratives in heritage

interpretation, see Russell Staiff, *Re-imagining Heritage Interpretation: Enchanting the Past-Future* (Farnham: Ashgate, 2014), 105.

[53] Mike Crang, "Rhythms of the City: Temporalised Space and Motion," in *Timespace: Geographies of Temporality*, ed. John May and Nigel Thrift (London: Routledge, 2001), 187–207 at 191 and 195.

[54] Mike Crang and Penny S. Travlou, "The City and Topologies of Memory," *Environment and Planning D: Society and Space* 19 (2001): 161–77 at 173.

[55] Henry Gastineau, "Swansea Harbour and Castle," in *Wales Illustrated in a Series of Views*, 2 vols. (London: Henry, Jones, 1830), 1:unpaginated. See also H. Griffith, *The New Swansea Guide; Containing a Particular Description of the Town and Its Vicinity: Together with a Short History of the County* (Swansea: H. Griffith, 1823), 60.

[56] County Borough of Swansea, Auxiliary Fire Service: Summary of Fires Attended–Enemy Action 21.2.41 / 22.2.41, fol. 6, Incident 45.

[57] Notice of the Making of a Declamatory Order: Plan and Schedule (Swansea, 12 August 1947), West Glamorgan Archives BE 52 / 15.

[58] G. B. Lewis, "Picture Essay: Swansea on the Map," in *The City of Swansea: Challenges and Change*, ed. Griffiths, 67–78 at 68; see also Map IX, p. 77.

[59] *Platea* has an extremely wide semantic range, but the *Dictionary of Medieval Latin from British Sources* gives its first sense as "street (usually in city or town [...] public as distinct from private space)." Rarely, it can refer to a cemetery and can also describe a "yard, court, courtyard, garden," though conventional usages again refer notably to secular spaces (Fascicule XI (2007), 2311–12).

[60] Michael Richter, "Waliser und Wundermänner um 1300," in *Spannungen und Widersprüche: Gedenkschrift für Frantisek Graus*, ed. S. Burghartz et al. (Sigmaringen: Thorbecke, 1992), 23–36 at 28.

[61] Sarah Rees Jones, "Civic Government and the Development of Public Buildings and Spaces in Later Medieval England," in *Construir la Ciudad en la Edad Media*, ed. B. A. Bolumburu and J. A. Solorzano Telechea (Logrono: IER, 2010), 497–512 at 497.

[62] D. M. Palliser et al., "The Topography of Towns 600–1300," in *The Cambridge Urban History of Britain*, ed. D. M. Palliser (Cambridge: Cambridge University Press, 2000), 153–86 at 160–68.

[63] G. B. Lewis, "Picture Essay: Swansea on the Map," 68.

[64] I am grateful to local residents of Swansea, who participated in the "City Witness" tour on Saturday, June 21, 2014, for sharing this information with me.

[65] Gerald Gabb, "How the Blitz Changed Swansea," *Minerva: Transactions of the Royal Institution of South Wales* 6 (1998): 21–30 at 25.

Winchester: Afterword

I'm in Winchester to prepare for a television documentary: an episode of the series *Britain's Most Historic Towns* (IWC Media for Channel 4 in the UK), which will feature the city as "Britain's Most Norman Town." The sequence I'm involved in will focus on the lost palace of William the Conqueror, so here I am, hunting for traces of the Normans in the heart of the modern city. As I walk through the streets, I'm re-tracing the paths of many other visitors and scholars, discovering fragments of history through a series of encounters with places, people, and the past.

In a chocolate shop on High Street, a wooden shelf unit laden with bags of truffles and arrays of brightly-wrapped bars partly obscures the medieval stonework on the back wall. But, unmistakably, there's a semi-circular Romanesque arch and a pillar, the wall around them filled with flintwork. The pillar is marooned up against much later brick, not obviously supporting anything very much—hints that this could be a fragment of masonry re-purposed and used in a new context. On the other side of this wall is the Church of St. Lawrence, built in the twelfth century on the site of the chapel royal of the Norman palace. The archway most likely dates from this mid-twelfth-century construction, and probably formed the original doorway onto the street. But the suggestive configuration of pillar and arch raises the possibility that this is medieval recycling: perhaps even the twelfth-century re-use of worked stone from the defunct Norman palace and chapel.

Round the corner, through the narrow passageway from the Butter Cross (a fifteenth-century market cross) to The Square, a large stone chimney breast also stands out conspicuously from the painted cement-rendered wall around it. A man who has been sleeping rough in the shelter of the passage points out to me a piece of decorative stone lower in the chimney breast: the block is worked into simple scallop shapes, overlapping like birds' feathers or the scales of a dragon. The opportunistic medieval inhabitant of Winchester who appropriated this stone for their chimney was, of course, far from unusual. Like Roman *spolia*, this Norman masonry likely served more than simply a structural function, the handsome stone and decorated panel carrying the prestige of history, even in the Middle Ages. While some forgotten burgess was collecting stone for his house here off High Street, Bishop Henry of Blois (Bishop of Winchester, 1129–71) was also engaged in enthusiastic recycling of the Norman palace's materials. When the Norman palace was heavily damaged in the Winchester siege of 1141—an episode in the "Anarchy" or civil war between the forces of King Stephen and the Empress Matilda—it had already become the residence of Bishop Henry, the main royal residence having moved to the larger castle at the south-west corner of the city. Gerald of Wales tells us that Henry—a "vir animosus et audax" ("spirited and audacious—or presumptuous—man") wasted no time in demolishing the remains of the Norman palace and arrogating the stone for his own houses, to the outrage of local people.[66]

A blue board on the outer wall of the tiny Church of St. Lawrence, its entrance tucked away along the passageway, declares: "BUILT UPON THE SITE OF THE CHAPEL ROYAL OF WILLIAM THE CONQUEROR." Most of the stone remains of William's chapel are invisible now, hidden in the foundations and also incorporated in one section of the east wall. But here is the other side of the rounded archway I saw in the chocolate shop and, high up on the west wall, a carved lion's head corbel (with a muzzle rather like a Saxon moustache) dates back to at least the twelfth century and perhaps, given its strangely de-contextualized placing (another hint of possible re-location), even earlier. Walking on, the basement of an upmarket gifts and clothing boutique reveals more medieval traces: Romanesque arches and vaulting, which I've never discovered before, having not ventured downstairs into the Menswear department. The shop assistant tells me that these are William the Conqueror's cellars, and that the mood changes down here when he's alone, at the end of the day, with a strange sense of something else close by, just out of sight.... Back across the Square and onto High Street, there are delicious smells wafting from a bakery and a pasty shop. The Winton Domesday (1110) tells us that near here was "unus vicus qui stupatus est pro coquina regis" ("a street which was blocked up for the king's kitchen").[67] Perhaps this is one final brush with the Norman palace: a teasing olfactory haunting from William the Conqueror's kitchens.

It is challenging to conjure a coherent, persuasive narrative for television out of these ambiguous remains and fragments, each of which are now something else, incorporated into other lives and stories of people and the city. As with any site of dense, continuous occupation, Winchester's history is one of re-use, re-appropriation, and transformation; the cityscape always folding its material into new configurations and meanings. The surviving medieval textual sources reflect this process of re-use and re-making. Even in the 1086 Great Domesday (which does not itself include a survey of Winchester), the entry for Kingsclere in Hampshire notes that the Abbey of St. Peter there holds lands given to it by King William, in exchange for land in Winchester, where now "domus regis est in civitate" ("the king's house is in the city"). Later, the 1110 Winton Domesday tells us about more than just the king's kitchens, giving further detail about the area off High Street cleared for the Norman palace—and the ordinary inhabitants of the city who had to make way. Lethmer (from the Old English *Leodmær*), Godwin the Frenchman, Sonric the hosier, and a woman called Edeva (Old English *Eadgifu*) are all included in the list of those who "tenebant domus et erant burgenses" ("held tenements and were burgesses") here. Their homes, along with the sites of five mints ("v mon-ete") were also cleared and the plots incorporated into William's palace. The Norman palace complex also included land from the cemetery of the New Minster, and was in sight of the pre-Conquest palace, which had been destroyed by fire around 1065.[68] The choice of this land speaks of more than simply expedient location: it represents the deliberate re-appropriation of Anglo-Saxon sites and symbols of power and authority in the early period of Norman rule.

While Winchester has its spectacular, splendid relics of the Middle Ages in its cathedral, the Great Hall of the castle, or even the impressive ruins of Henry of Blois' palace at Wolvesey, the meaning of the fragments of the Norman palace is much less clear. Yet they dramatize, in intriguing and lively ways, the complex and messy relationships between time and place in the medieval cityscape today. The partial, jumbled pieces of William the Conqueror's palace might, perhaps, help to animate our understanding of temporality and the historic environment, as well as the theoretical discourses which are currently emerging, especially in Medieval and Medievalist Studies, to articulate freshly-nuanced versions of the relationships between time, place, and individual experience. Some of these approaches are explicitly influenced by concepts of queer temporalities, and other work in recent decades which resists linear models of chronology or historical time (themselves largely post-medieval constructs) and which explore other, more diverse experiences of temporality. Carolyn Dinshaw's book *How Soon is Now? Medieval Texts, Amateur Readers, and the Queerness of Time* (2012) was a landmark book in bringing these theories of queer temporalities into Medieval Studies, examining fundamental intersections between time and desire in relation to the medieval past. Dinshaw explores "multiple temporalities," "asynchronies," and "temporal heterogeneity," and suggests that the experience of "amateurs" might afford different—and potentially more dynamic or capacious—modes of connection with diverse moments in and models of time than the practice of the professional academic historian.

Dinshaw's work on the queerness of time is present in the genealogy of another recent theoretical approach which seeks to articulate the complex relationships between moments in time, especially in place. The term "distemporality" has been used by a number of scholars to express moments of suggestive, productive apposition or dissonance between past and present, including especially "[m]oments [...] of uncanniness, of error, or of a return to sense [that] occur in pauses [...] or tiny details of interruptive anachronisms as the 'now' folds and multiplies."[69] Recently, Jonathan Hsy has brought the notion of distemporality to his study of the media narratives and public reception surrounding the sensational discovery of Richard III's body in a Leicester carpark in 2012. Hsy articulates the powerful apposition between the body of a medieval monarch and a modern-day parking lot in terms of "a feeling of collision, explosion": a dynamic harnessed to powerful effect in the 2016 National Theatre production of Shakespeare's *Richard III*, starring Ralph Fiennes, which began and ended with that hole in the tarmac, and workmen in hard hats. Where queer time is intrinsically bound up with notions of desire—as Hsy puts it, "flowing circuits of desire, contact, affective cross-identification across historical periods"—distemporality is characterized by moments of abrasive, explosive apposition, in which heterogeneous chronological moments "jostle."[70] While "distemporality" foregrounds dynamics of desire less emphatically than models of queer time, it serves well the uncanny, disruptive—often funny—juxtapositions encountered in the historic environment, as exemplified in the recycled remains of William the Conqueror's palace in Winchester, or the many other strange appositions in Rouen, Chester, and Swansea explored in this volume.

Theories of queer time resonate powerfully with the experience of medieval remains in cities today for many people: the desire to find a means of immediate sensory and affective connection with a remote historical past; the wish to "step into history" and experience the pleasures of contact between past and present. The aesthetic desire which arrests the urban environment into a "cityscape"—a static and coherent prospect—is fundamentally different from the queerer, stranger longings for affective contact with remote, other, past moments and lives which animate the historic city for many individuals today. As the site of powerful cross-currents of time and desire, the city becomes, rather, a space of folded temporalities and shifting, elusive glimpses, in which disparate historical moments are willed into proximity. "Heritage," of course, relies on the mobilization of affect and desire, transforming "history" into a version of the past contingent on subjective individual perspective and identification. The queerness of some of those desires, in their impulses to transgress chronological propriety and seek out strange, trans-historical affinities, perhaps deserves greater acknowledgement and exploration in analyses of engagement with historic environments today. New digital tools, augmented reality applications and virtual experiences offer ways of amplifying and extending those partial, fragmentary experiences of the past, as well as ways of making strange the embodied experience of being in a place—often inviting participants to inhabit an alternative identity or historical moment, or to see with new eyes.

The historic urban environment today is an expanding space, enlarging to encompass versions of the past desired, sought, and recuperated by diverse communities, as well as the various realms—material, conceptual, and digital (virtual or hybrid)—which increasingly constitute it. These emerging possibilities offer exciting new ways of working for those engaged in heritage management or conservation, as well as for those in the academy exploring intersections between place and history. More than ever, tools and technologies exist which allow scholars of the historic city to make interventions in the urban environment today, in ways which go far beyond factual interpretation or physical conservation to include playful re-imaginings, creative, subjective, and experimental responses, and virtual transformations. Whether visible or invisible, familiar or hidden, medieval history is a key part of the landscape of many of our towns and cities. Scholars in traditional Humanities disciplines—every bit as much as those working in heritage science, tourism studies, or in applied and practitioner contexts—have the opportunity to shape the presentation and public understanding of historic urban environments today, and to participate in the production of a rich, meaningful, and culturally-legible public realm.

Notes

[66] Giraldus Cambrensis, *Opera*, vol. 7, *Vita S. Remigii*, ed. J. F. Dimmock (London: Rolls Series, 1877), 7:45 (chap. 27).

[67] Martin Biddle, ed., Winton Domesday, Survey I (60) in *Winchester in the Early Middle Ages*, Winchester Studies, 1 (Oxford: Clarendon Press, 1976), 43.

[68] For the relevant Domesday entries see *Winchester in the Early Middle Ages*, Survey I (110), entries 57–60; for discussion of the location of the Norman palace see pp. 292–302.

[69] Rebecca Schneider, *Performing Remains: Art and War in Times of Theatrical Reenactment* (New York: Routledge, 2011), 186.

[70] Jonathan Hsy, "Distemporality: Richard III's Body and the Car Park," *Upstart: A Journal of English Renaissance Studies* (2013) (online only).

Further Reading

The Medieval City

Two key starting points for investigating the history and material heritage of towns and cities today are the Victoria County History (for England), based at the Institute of Historical Research, University of London (https://www.victoriacountyhistory.ac.uk/); and the Historic Towns Atlas project, in the United Kingdom (http://www.historictownsatlas.org.uk/) and in Europe (http://www.uni-muenster.de/Staedtegeschichte/en/portal/staedteatlanten/karte.html).

Cityscape / Townscape

Comment, Bernard. *The Panorama*. London: Reaktion, 1999.
> History of the panorama as artform, and its role in shaping visions and ideals of the cityscape.

Hyde, Ralph. *A Prospect of Britain: The Town Panoramas of Samuel and Nathaniel Buck*. London: Pavilion, 1994.
> Edition of these hugely influential eighteenth-century prospect views of towns and cities, formative to ideals of the urban landscape.

The Iconography of Landscape. Edited by Denis Cosgrove and Stephen Daniels. Cambridge: Cambridge University Press: 1988.
> A collection of essays exploring landscape as cultural image.

Ottermann, Stephan. *The Panorama: History of a Mass Medium*. Cambridge, MA: MIT Press, 1977.
> Another history of the panorama as spectacle (translated from the German, originally published in 1990).

Heritage Debates

The Ashgate Research Companion to Heritage and Identity. Edited by B. Graham and P. Howard. Aldershot: Ashgate, 2008.

> A great starting-point for exploring key themes, theories, and practices relating to heritage.

Ashworth, G. J. "From History to Heritage: From Heritage to Identity: In Search of Concepts and Models." In *Building a New Heritage: Tourism, Culture and Identity in the New Europe*, edited by G. J. Ashworth and P. J. Larkham, 13–30. London: Routledge, 1994.

> A touchstone paper examining the ways in which history is commodified as heritage, and how the past can provide raw materials for heritage tourism and economic development and place-making.

Goulding, Christina. "Romancing the Past: Heritage Visiting and the Nostalgic Consumer." *Psychology and Marketing* 18 (2001): 565–92.

> This essay explores the intersections between history, nostalgia, and heritage "consumption."

Lowenthal, David. *The Past is a Foreign Country—Revisited.* Cambridge: Cambridge University Press, 2015.

> A landmark book from a figure key to the formation of Heritage Studies as a field, and a major voice in critiques of heritage practice, consumption, and politics.

——. "The Past as a Theme Park." In *Theme Park Landscapes: Antecedents and Variations*, edited by Terence Young and Robert Riley, 11–24. Washington: Dumbarton Oaks, 2002.

> In this essay, Lowenthal examines the commodification of historic landscapes for heritage consumers today.

Urry, John. *The Tourist Gaze 3.0.* Los Angeles: SAGE, 2011.

> The most recent edition of this seminal work, analyzing and theorizing tourism behaviours and practices from a sociological perspective.

Theoretical and Conceptual Approaches

Butterfield, Ardis. "Chaucer and the Detritus of the City." In *Chaucer and the City*, edited by Ardis Butterfield, 3–24. Cambridge: Brewer, 2006.

> An imaginative essay which finds a way into Chaucer's city through an art installation at Tate Modern and the detritus of fourteenth-century London.

Camille, Michel. *The Gargoyles of Notre Dame: Medievalism and the Monsters of Modernity*. Chicago: University of Chicago Press, 2009.

> This case study takes the nineteenth-century "medieval" gargoyles of Notre Dame, Paris, as a starting-point for thinking about material and conceptual medievalisms.

Coverley, Merlin. *Psychogeography*. Harpenden: Pocket Essentials, 2006.

> A useful point of entry into the diverse literary and cultural histories of "psychogeography" as a mode of engaging imaginatively with place.

Crang, Mike. "Rhythms of the City: Temporalised Space and Motion." In *Timespace: Geographies of Temporality*, edited by John May and Nigel Thrift, 187–207. London: Routledge, 2001.

> A theoretical approach, from an influential cultural geographer, to time, temporalities, and space in urban environments.

De Certeau, Michel. *The Practice of Everyday Life*. Translated by Steven Rendall. Berkeley: University of California Press, 1988.

> Theoretical approaches formative to much recent work on urban environments and experiences, including the highly influential chapter "Walking in the City," with its account of the city both viewed from above and "made" by practitioners in the streets.

Lilley, Keith D. *City and Cosmos: The Medieval World in Urban Form*. London: Reaktion, 2009.

> A key work on cities in the medieval imagination, paying attention to their symbolic properties.

Salih, Sarah. "In/visible Medieval/isms." *Studies in Medievalism* 25 (2016): 53–70.

> Salih's quest for the medieval London Stone folds in multiple temporal layers, diverse sources, and personal experience, to explore history "on the verge of visibility."

Strohm, Paul. *Theory and the Premodern Text*. Minneapolis: University of Minnesota Press, 2000.

> The chapter "Three London Itineraries" builds on Henri LeFebvre's theories of the production of space to examine the meanings of medieval London through journeys made by Chaucer, Usk, and Hoccleve.

Conservation and Reconstruction

Beckwith, Sarah. "Preserving, Conserving, Deserving the Past: A Meditation on Ruin as Relic in Postwar Britain." In *A Place to Believe In: Locating Medieval Landscapes*, edited by Clare Lees and Gillian Overing. University Park: Pennsylvania State University Press, 2006.

   A wide-ranging exploration of cultural representations and uses of the ruin in Britain after 1945.

Bandarin, Francesco, and Ron van Oers. *The Historic Urban Landscape: Managing Heritage in an Urban Century*. Oxford: Blackwell, 2014.

   An overview of recent policies, practices, and trends in the management and conservation of urban heritage, with particular reference to UNESCO perspectives.

Larkham, Peter J., and Keith D. Lilley. "Townscape and Scenography: Conceptualizing and Communicating the New Urban Landscape in British Post-War Planning." In *Alternative Visions of Post-War Reconstruction*, edited by John Pendlebury et al. Abingdon: Routledge, 2015.

   This article looks at the representation of planned and imagined urban landscapes in post-war Britain, with close attention to relationships between imagery and cultural or political ideals.

Lilley, K. D. "Modern Visions of the Medieval City: Competing Conceptions of Urbanism in European Civic Design." *Environment and Planning B: Planning and Design* 26 (1999): 427–46.

   Lilley explores how many twentieth-century urban designs were influenced by ideas of the medieval city.

Pendlebury, John. "Planning the Historic City: Reconstruction Plans in the United Kingdom in the 1940s." *Town Planning Review* 73 (2004): 371–93.

   An examination of how post-war planners negotiated between radical new visions for reconstructing urban centres and recognition of the value of historic sites and fabric.

Technology

The London Charter for the Computer-based Visualisation of Heritage 2.1. http://www.londoncharter.org/, 2009.

   An important document, developed by a consortium of academics and practitioners, which is an example of an attempt to articulate best practice in the digital visualization of heritage.

Mixed Reality and Gamification for Cultural Heritage. Edited by Marinos Ioannides, Nadia Magnenat-Thalmann, and George Papagiannakis. Cham: Springer, 2017.

> These essays offer a wide-ranging overview of theories, technologies, and applications in the presentation of cultural heritage through augmented reality or game-led models.

The Virtual Representation of the Past. Edited by Mark Greengrass and Lorna Hughes. Farnham: Ashgate, 2008.

> Brings together diverse viewpoints on the virtual representation of the past through digital media.

Visualization in Archaeology. http://archaeologydataservice.ac.uk/archives/view/via_eh_2014/, 2014.

> This online report was the outcome of a major three-year project exploring practical and theoretical aspects of the visual presentation of archaeological knowledge, with particular attention to digital methods.

Time and Temporality

DeLanda, Manuel. *A Thousand Years of Nonlinear History*. New York: Zone, 2000.

> A provocative book which offers radical, revisionist approaches to concepts including history, materiality, and the urban.

Dinshaw, Carolyn. *How Soon is Now? Medieval Texts, Amateur Readers, and the Queerness of Time*. Durham: Duke University Press, 2012.

> A major contribution to current debates, often led by medievalists, about non-linear or "queer," "asynchronies," and "temporal heterogeneity," shaped in part through careful attention to the affective dimensions of amateur engagement with the past.

Chester

Barrett Jr., Robert W. *Against all England: Regional Identity and Cheshire Writing, 1195–1656*. Notre Dame: University of Notre Dame Press, 2009.

> A rigorous and nuanced examination of local identities and cultural production in medieval and early-modern Cheshire, showing the complex ways in which local and national identities are interlaced in place.

Discover Medieval Chester. http.discover.medievalchester.ac.uk, 2013.

> A public-facing website interpreting medieval Chester for modern communities and visitors, including an interactive tour map and multi-media resources, as well as a gallery showing the St John's art installation.

Mapping Medieval Chester: Place and Identity in an English Border-land City c.1200–1500. www.medievalchester.ac.uk, 2009.

> Website produced by the "Mapping Medieval Chester" project, bringing together medieval textual "mappings" of the city in English, Latin, and Welsh with a digital atlas of Chester ca. 1500. *Mapping the*

Medieval City: Space, Place and Identity in Chester c.1200–1600. Edited by Catherine A. M. Clarke. Cardiff: University of Wales Press, 2011.

> This book emerged from the "Mapping Medieval Chester" project and brings together diverse inter-disciplinary perspectives on place and identity in the medieval city.

The Rows of Chester: The Chester Rows Research Project. Edited by Andrew Brown. English Heritage Archaeological Report 16 (1999).

> Key source for understanding the history of Chester's famous Rows, both medieval and post-medieval.

Ward, S. W. "The Archaeology of Medieval Chester: A Review." *Journal of the Chester Archaeological Society* 73 (1994–95): 3–62.

> An excellent overview from the Principal Archaeologist at Cheshire West and Chester local authority.

Swansea

City Witness: Place and Perspective in Medieval Swansea. www.medievalswansea.ac.uk, 2014.

> This website brings together the first edition and translation of the nine eyewitness statements describing the hanging of William Cragh in 1290, with an interactive map of the medieval town, and a range of varied visualisations. The site also includes an interactive tour map with multi-media interpretation content.

Clarke, Catherine A. M., ed. "Power, Identity and Miracles on a Medieval Frontier." Special Issue, *Journal of Medieval History* 41 (2015).

> Includes articles on spatial practices in medieval Swansea, processes involved in mapping and interpreting the historic townscape, and other perspectives on cultural and political contexts.

Hanska, Jussi. "The Hanging of William Cragh: Anatomy of a Miracle." *Journal of Medieval History* 27 (2001): 121–38.

   A key study into the strange case of "hanged man" William Cragh.

Morris, Bernard. "From Swansea Castle to Gibbet Hill." *Minerva: The Swansea History Journal* 18 (2010-11): 6–11.

   A leading historian of Swansea explores the story of William Cragh in the spatial context of the medieval town.

Robinson, W. R. B. "Medieval Swansea." In *Glamorgan County History*, vol. 3, *The Middle Ages*, edited by T. B. Pugh, 361–77. Cardiff: Glamorgan County History Society, 1971.

   An indispensable overview of the history and development of medieval Swansea.

——. "Medieval Swansea." In *Boroughs of Mediaeval Wales*, edited by R. A. Griffiths, 263–88. Cardiff: University of Wales Press, 1978.

   Another key account of the medieval history and development of Swansea.

Soulsby, Ian. *Towns of Medieval Wales*. Chichester: Phillimore, 1983.

   An excellent overview, bringing together documentary and archaeological evidence.

Oxford: 'Rethinking States, Nations & Constitutions in the 21st Century' and 'The Nation State and the International Order: Constitutions, Revolutions, Security & Global Sources of Law'. He has also published through the Foundation for Law, Justice and Society a case study of court enforcement of socio-economic rights, based on his 'Homeless Families with Children' litigation regarding the right to shelter.

Anna Coote is a leading analyst, writer and advocate in the field of social policy. She is Principal Fellow at the New Economics Foundation. She was Commissioner for Health with the UK Sustainable Development Commission (2000–9), led the Healthcare Commission's work on engaging patients and the public (2005–8) and was Director of Health Policy at the King's Fund (1998–2004).

Earlier posts include Senior Research Fellow and Deputy Director of IPPR (1989–98), Editor and Producer of Current Affairs Television for Diverse Productions (1982–6) and Deputy Editor of the *New Statesman* (1978–82). She has written widely on social policy, sustainable development, public health policy, public involvement and democratic dialogue, gender and equality. Her recent publications for NEF include

Local Early Action: How to Make it Happen (2015), *The Wrong Medicine: A Review of the Impacts of NHS Reforms* (2015), *People, Planet, Power: Towards a New Social Settlement* (2015) and *Time on Our Side: Why We All Need a Shorter Working Week* (2013).

Anne Deighton is Professor of European International Politics at the University of Oxford. She is based in the Department of Politics and International Relations, and the Faculty of History in the University of Oxford, where she works on themes relating to contemporary history, international relations and to the political integration of Europe.

Her major writing project is a political biography of Ernest Bevin, British Foreign Secretary in the 1940s. She has published extensively on European security institutions; the genesis of international human rights issues in postwar Europe; and the use, and abuse, of military force in the contemporary world.

Michael Dougan is Head of Law and Professor of European Law, University of Liverpool. He specializes in EU Law, particularly EU constitutional and institutional law, legal relations between the EU and its member states, the law of the single market and free movement of persons/EU welfare law. Michael is Joint Editor of *Common Market Law Review* – the world's leading scientific journal for European legal research.

Michael has published articles in journals such as the *European Law Review*, *European Public Law* and *Cambridge Yearbook of European Legal Studies*. He is the author of *National Remedies before the Court of Justice* (2004) and the co-editor of various collections of essays and special journal issues. He is a co-author of Wyatt & Dashwood's *EU Law* (6th edn, 2011) – one of the leading English-language authorities in the field.

Sionaidh Douglas-Scott joined Queen Mary University of London (QMUL) in September 2015 as Anniversary Chair in Law and Co-Director of the Centre for Law and Society in a Global Context. Prior to this, she was Professor of European and Human Rights Law at the University of Oxford, and before that Professor of Law at King's College London.

Professor Douglas-Scott works primarily within the fields of constitutional law, EU public law, human rights and legal and social theory, and is particularly interested in questions of justice and human rights in Europe. She has published widely in these fields, including *Constitutional Law of the European Union*. She is also interested in substate independence movements in Europe and has been an active commentator on Scottish and Catalan independence movements in the media, as well as giving expert evidence to the Westminster and Scottish Parliaments on further Scottish devolution.

D.J. Galligan is Professor of Socio-Legal Studies, and a Professorial Fellow of Wolfson College, University of Oxford. Professor Galligan is a member of the Board of Directors of the Foundation for Law, Justice and Society, an independent institution affiliated with the Centre for Socio-Legal Studies and based at Wolfson College, University of Oxford. His books include *Law in Modern Society*, *Western Concepts of Administrative Law*, *Due Process and Fair Procedures* and *Discretionary Powers*.

Timothy Garton Ash is Professor of European Studies in the University of Oxford, Isaiah Berlin Professorial Fellow at St Antony's College, Oxford, and Senior Fellow at the Hoover Institution, Stanford University. He is the author of ten books of political writing or 'history of the present' including *The Magic Lantern: The Revolution of '89 Witnessed in Warsaw, Budapest, Berlin, & Prague*;

The File: A Personal History; *In Europe's Name* and *Facts are Subversive.*

He writes a column on international affairs in the *Guardian*, which is widely syndicated, and is a regular contributor to the *New York Review of Books*, among other journals. He leads the 13-language Oxford University research project Freespeechdebate.com, and his latest book is *Free Speech: Ten Principles for a Connected World*. Awards he has received for his writing include the George Orwell Prize. In January 2017 he was awarded the Karlspreis (Charlemagne Prize) for his work on European unification.

A.C. Grayling is Master of the New College of the Humanities, London, and its Professor of Philosophy, and the author of over 30 books of philosophy, biography, history of ideas, and essays. He is a columnist for *Prospect* magazine, and was for a number of years a columnist on the *Guardian* and *Times*. He has contributed to many leading newspapers in the UK, US and Australia, and to BBC Radio 4, 3, 2 and the World Service, for which he did the annual *Exchanges at the Frontier* series; and he has often appeared on television.

He has twice been a judge on the Booker Prize, in 2015 serving as the chair of the judging panel. He is Vice

President of the British Humanist Association, Fellow of the Royal Society of Arts and Fellow of the Royal Society of Literature.

Robert Hazell CBE is Professor of Government and the Constitution at University College London. He founded the Constitution Unit at UCL in 1995 as an independent think tank specializing in constitutional reform. The Unit has published detailed reports on every aspect of Britain's constitutional reform programme: devolution, the Human Rights Act, parliamentary reform, Lords reform, freedom of information, referendums and electoral reform.

Professor Hazell's last three books have been on the Conservative–Liberal Democrat coalition; special advisers; and the politics of judicial independence. In early 2016 he helped to organize a series of seminars on the implications of Brexit, and is currently trying to raise funding for an independent Referendums Commission. Before founding the Constitution Unit he had three previous careers: as a barrister (1973–5), a civil servant in the Home Office (1975–89) and Director of the Nuffield Foundation (1989–95). In 2006 he was awarded the CBE for his services to constitutional reform.

Philip Kay combines a career in finance with academic research. Having held senior positions at Schroders, Smith New Court and Credit Suisse, he is now the managing partner of a specialist Japanese asset management firm.

He is also Supernumerary Fellow of Wolfson College, Oxford, where his main research interests include the economy of the Roman Republic, the structure and practice of ancient banking and the socio-economic context of early Roman law. He is the author of *Rome's Economic Revolution* (2014).

Michael Keating is Professor of Politics at the universities of Aberdeen and Edinburgh and Director of the Centre on Constitutional Change. He graduated from the University of Oxford and in 1975 was the first PhD graduate from what is now Glasgow Caledonian University. Michael is a fellow of the British Academy, Royal Society of Edinburgh, Academy of Social Sciences and European Academy and has taught in universities in Scotland, England, Canada, the USA, France and Spain and at the European University Institute in Italy.

Among his publications are *Plurinational Democracy* (2001); *The Independence of Scotland* (2009) and

Rescaling the European State (2013). His edited book, *Debating Scotland*, an analysis of the 2014 referendum debate, was published in February 2017.

Mark Knights is Professor of History at the University of Warwick. He has written about early modern Britain and is the author of *Representation and Misrepresentation in Later Stuart Britain: Partisanship and Political Culture* (2007). His most recent book is *The Devil in Disguise: Deception, Delusion and Fanaticism in the Early English Enlightenment* (2011). He is currently writing a book about corruption in Britain and its colonies from the sixteenth-century reformation to nineteenth-century reform.

He writes a blog about corruption past and present at http://blogs.warwick.ac.uk/historyofcorruption/ and has published a report about the history of corruption for Transparency International at http://www.transparency. org.uk/publications/old-corruption-what-british-history-can-tell-us-about-corruption-today/.

Jonathan Lis is Deputy Director of British Influence (formally the Centre for British Influence Through Europe), a pro-single market foreign affairs think tank. Jonathan read English at Trinity College, Cambridge before completing a master's degree in social sciences at the London School of Economics.

In 2012, Jonathan became the senior assistant to Charles Tannock MEP, the Conservative coordinator on foreign affairs and human rights at the European Parliament. Following a period working for the Unrepresented Nations and Peoples Organisation, Jonathan began working with British Influence, and wrote its pre-referendum report on Brexit and the Commonwealth. As part of the organization's work on the single market, Jonathan conceived of the legal challenge regarding Britain's apparent automatic withdrawal from the European Economic Area, which was brought before the courts in February 2017.

Rob Murray is the lead partner for Mishcon de Reya LLP representing the lead claimant, Gina Miller, in proceedings against the Secretary of State for exiting the EU in relation to the service of notice to leave under Article 50 of the Treaty of Lisbon.

Rob has represented clients in leading competition damages claims in the English High Court and the Competition Appeal Tribunal (CAT). He is ranked as a Leading Individual for Competition Litigation in Legal 500 2015 and Chambers & Partners 2016. Rob has also advised businesses in making complaints to national competition regulators and DGComp of the European Commission.

Canon Ailsa Newby has been, from 2010 until her appointment in 2017 as Canon Pastor at Ripon Cathedral, Team Rector in the Parish of Putney based at St Mary's Church, a large church in the Liberal Catholic tradition of the Church of England and site of the original Putney Debates in 1647.

Prior to ordination Ailsa worked first in the City of London as a solicitor and later as a Legal Officer at the law reform and human rights organization JUSTICE, where she specialized in miscarriage of justice cases and criminal law reform, and worked on the submission of evidence to select committees and the Law Commission. At St Mary's, she worked to promote the Putney Debates heritage of the church.

John Rees is a writer, broadcaster and activist, and author of *The Leveller Revolution*, which is based on his doctoral research at Goldsmiths, University of London, where he is now Visiting Research Fellow.

His previous books include *Timelines, A Political History of the Modern World, Imperialism and Resistance* and *A People's History of London* (with Lindsey German). He is the co-founder of the Stop the War Coalition and a spokesperson for the People's Assembly. He is currently editing a collection of essays on the Leveller leader John Lilburne.

Linda Risso is Senior Fellow at the Institute of Historical Research in London. She is an expert on the history of European defence and security in the twentieth century. Dr Risso works on the historical development of the European Union and of NATO, and – more broadly – on the legacies of the Cold War on today's security and strategic thinking.

David Runciman is a political theorist at the University of Cambridge where he is Head of the Department of Politics and International Studies (POLIS). He has worked as a columnist for the *Guardian* newspaper and written for many other publications.

He currently writes about politics for the *London Review of Books*. Professor Runciman's latest book, *Politics: Ideas in Profile*, asks the big questions about politics: what is it, why we do we need it and where, in these turbulent times, is it heading? His research interests include: late nineteenth- and twentieth-century political thought; theories of the state and of political representation; various aspects of contemporary political philosophy and contemporary politics.

Alexandra Runswick is Director of Unlock Democracy. She started her career working on feminist and environmental campaigns and increasing public participation in healthcare, before moving to democratic reform. She has over ten years' experience of parliamentary and grassroots campaigning on issues such as lobbying transparency, party funding, freedom of information, House of Lords reform, electoral reform, women's representation in politics and participatory democracy.

She has published pamphlets on party funding reform, including *Party Funding – Supporting the Grassroots* and *Life Support for Local Parties*, and worked with the British Council to produce *People and Policy-making – A Guide for Political Parties*, a resource for local political parties on how they can involve the public in policymaking.

Philip Schofield is Professor of the History of Legal and Political Thought in the Faculty of Laws and Director of the Bentham Project, University College London.

He is General Editor of the new authoritative edition of *The Collected Works of Jeremy Bentham*, for which he has edited or co-edited around a dozen volumes. His major study *Utility and Democracy: The Political Thought of Jeremy Bentham*, was published in 2006.

Sir Stephen Sedley was called to the Bar (Inner Temple) in 1964 and practised for 28 years, specializing in public law and discrimination law. He was involved in many high-profile cases and inquiries, from the death of Blair Peach and the Carl Bridgewater murder trial to the contempt hearing against Kenneth Baker, then Home Secretary.

He became a QC in 1983, and was appointed a High Court judge in 1992, serving in the Queen's Bench Division. In 1999 Stephen Sedley was appointed to the Court of Appeal as a Lord Justice of Appeal. He has sat on the Judicial Committee of the Privy Council and as a judge ad hoc of the European Court of Human Rights. He also chaired the Judicial Studies Board's working party on the Human Rights Act 1998 and was, from 1999 until 2012, President of the British Institute of Human Rights. He also helped to establish the Public Law Project, a UK charity concerned with access to justice and social exclusion, and is a Trustee of the Equal Rights Trust.

Sir Richard Sorabji is a philosopher and historian of ancient Western philosophy, and Honorary Fellow of Wolfson College, Oxford. He is the author of 16 books and editor of over 100 translations of Greek philosophy, with the aid of 300 collaborators in 20 countries.

Professor Sorabji founded the King's College Centre for Philosophical Studies between 1989 and 1991, with the aim of promoting philosophy to the wider public, and was Director of the Institute of Classical Studies from 1991 to 1996. He was appointed Commander of the Order of the British Empire (CBE) in 1999 for his services to ancient philosophy, and knighted in 2014 for services to philosophical scholarship. He became a fellow of the British Academy in 1989.

David Vines is Director of the Political Economy of Financial Markets Programme at St Antony's College, Oxford, and was formally Professor of Economics, and Fellow of Balliol College, at the University of Oxford. He is also Research Fellow of the Centre for Economic Policy Research.

From 2008 to 2012 he was Research Director of the European Union's Framework Seven PEGGED Research Program, which analysed Global Economic Governance within Europe. His research interests are in macroeconomics, financial regulation and global economic governance, and include studying the interaction of fiscal policy and monetary policy, and the effects of financial crises. His recent books include *Keynes: Useful Economics for the World Economy* (with Peter Temin); *The Leaderless Economy: Why the World Economic System Fell Apart and How to Fix It* (with Peter Temin) and *Capital Failure: Rebuilding Trust in Financial Services* (with Nicholas Morris).

Alison Young is Professor of Public Law at the University of Oxford and Fellow and Tutor in Law at Hertford College.

She is the author of *Democratic Dialogue and the Constitution* (2017) and *Parliamentary Sovereignty and the Human Rights Act* (2009), as well as publishing widely on public law and human rights.

Acknowledgements

This small volume is a record of the Putney Debates that took place in St Mary's Church in Putney on 2–3 February 2017. The Debates were organized by the Foundation for Law, Justice and Society (FLJS), an independent institute dedicated to promoting better understanding of the role of law in society, based at Wolfson College and affiliated with the Centre for Socio-Legal Studies at the University of Oxford. The Debates also benefited from the generous support of the Faculty of Law at the University of Oxford.

We thank Mr John Adams, Chairman of the Foundation for Law, Justice and Society, and other members of the Board of Trustees for their support. Without the dedication of Judy Niner and Phil Dines at the Foundation, the event would not have taken place. We also thank the small group of Oxford students whose assistance during the two days of the Debates was invaluable.

St Mary's Church, Putney, the site of the original Putney Debates in 1647, proved the perfect place in which to deliberate on matters of constitution. We give warm thanks to Canon Ailsa Newby for allowing use of St Mary's and for taking part in the Debates, and to the staff of St Mary's, who provided most helpful support over the two days, and who continue to support the Debates by making available copies of this collected volume at the Church.

To the Debaters, all 33 of them, and the Chairs, who travelled to Putney from across the nation, we are much indebted. The range and diversity of views on display, together with the authority with which they were expressed, made the occasion. To hear the views of scholars and lawyers, historians and philosophers, businesspeople and financiers, to name just some of the professional backgrounds, was a rich and rare experience. That each speaker was limited to five minutes, a rule generally respected, ensured a degree of concentration and concision not often encountered. Such an approach has resulted in a series of contributions over the ensuing pages that are distinguished both by their brevity and their breadth of insight, which we hope will appeal to the committed constitutionalist and the concerned citizen alike.

Lastly, credit goes to Joanna Godfrey, Senior Editor at I.B.Tauris, for identifying the Debates as ripe for wider dissemination through the publication of this collected volume. Our thanks go to Joanna and her colleague Sara Magness for their professionalism and perseverance in guiding the book along an impressively expeditious publication schedule. We hope that this collected volume will, in its modest way, serve the present thirst for intelligent prognosis of the state of the nation's health, and that it will inform and extend the ongoing public debate on the UK's constitutional future.

Introduction

D.J. Galligan

The Putney Debates 1647

On 25 October 1647, the *Moderate Intelligencer*, a 'newsbook' of the day, reported: 'A great assembly was this day at Putney Church, where was debated matters of high concernment.' What the matters of high concernment were, the *Moderate Intelligencer* did not say. We now know that they were indeed matters of high concernment. The civil war was over, the king in captivity, Parliament in disarray. The New Model Army was effectively in control, while the Levellers, a reforming political movement, in today's parlance plainly populist, were gathering support. The balanced constitution, balanced among king, peers and commons, had been destroyed.

The weekly meeting of the General Council of the New Model Army, on 28 October 1647, although not so intended, turned into a debate over fundamental matters of constitution. Stretching over several days, the meeting turned into a constitutional convention of a kind and importance not seen since.

As the debate took its course, two competing notions of constitution became plain. One is based on the old balanced constitution, with suitable adjustments in favour of the House of Commons at the cost of reduction of the king's powers. This was the constitution founded on property, class divisions and rule by those who know best how to rule. The other notion was visionary; it foresaw a new constitutional order without king or peers; a sovereign people, with wider voting rights and a House of Commons restricted in its powers and accountable to the people. Even the common people – Cromwell's 'mere breathers', Shakespeare's 'mechanicals' – would have their rights protected and some say in how they were to be governed.

As the differences became clear, attitudes hardened and the gap between the two sides became unbridgeable. The debate ended without agreement. Cromwell soon after assumed authority: the king was tried, convicted and executed; the Commonwealth was launched; and the rest is history. But it lasted little more than a decade, after which the monarchy was restored, the old balanced constitution reinstated, with some adjustments in favour of the Commons. From that constitutional settlement, our own is the direct descendant.

The Constitutional Issues for Debate

David Hume, the philosopher, historian and social theorist, writing in the eighteenth century, observed:

> Nothing appears more surprising to those who consider human affairs with a philosophical eye, than the ease with which the many are governed by the few; and the implicit submission, with which men resign their own sentiments to those of their rulers.

Hume went on to say that it is all the more curious when you consider that power, raw power, is always on the side of the governed, for 'the governors have nothing to support them but opinion. It is therefore, on opinion only that government is founded'.

That is the central issue for a constitution, for constitutional authority: the relationship between rulers and ruled, between government and the people. What reasons do the majority have for restraining their natural liberty and accepting, or acquiescing in, a system of authority from which they may feel excluded or with which they are in disagreement? Various explanations have been advanced, some based on religious precepts, others on moral duty. The notion of a social contract was prominent in Hume's day, the idea being that the people enter into a contract among themselves to appoint government and then accept its authority. Unpersuaded by any of these accounts, Hume took a more pragmatic approach based on two propositions: one, that the people are naturally inclined to accept the system of constitutional authority that happens to be in place; the other, that government is necessary for providing some of the necessities of life, such as protection of personal and property rights, the enforceability of contracts and general security.

Our present concern, however, is not so much with the ends of constitutional government and the reasons people acquiesce, but with the institutions through which such acquiescence is achieved in the United Kingdom. The system of authority in which we acquiesce is the sovereignty of Parliament, as the Supreme Court reaffirmed earlier this year. It means: Parliament has the authority to make or unmake any law. Parliament means the two Houses of Parliament and the monarch.

The two houses normally have to agree on proposed legislation, although in case of irreconcilable disagreement, the House of Commons may have its will. Once a bill has met the requirements of the two houses, the Queen gives her assent, normally as a matter of course, although in certain exceptional cases she may have discretion to refuse. In light of the restrictions on the House of Lords and the monarch, in reality, parliamentary sovereignty means the sovereignty of the House of Commons.

Parliamentary sovereignty was established by parliamentarians in the eighteenth century, to whose fragmented ideas William Blackstone gave form and authority, which A.V. Dicey endorsed in the later nineteenth century and which remain, in essence, the doctrine we have today.

Parliamentary sovereignty is founded upon and justified by the representative principle: Parliament represents the people and acts on their behalf. The relationship between Parliament the representative, and the people as represented, has two enduring features: firstly, it is one of inherent tension; secondly, it is dynamic and changeable. The tension is due to the artificial line drawn between what is for the people and what is for Parliament. It is dynamic and changeable because the line depends on opinion, and opinion moves and shifts with the social and political climate of the times.

The Putney Debates 2017

Today, in 2017, we also have matters of 'high concernment' to debate; we also find ourselves undergoing a period of constitutional tension and a shifting political climate. Once again, following the UK's Referendum on membership of the European Union in 2016, the oldest and most critical feature of a constitutional order is thrown into question: the place of the people and their relationship with the institutions of government. The relationship, as David Hume expressed it, between the few who rule and the many who are ruled.

The purpose of the Foundation for Law, Justice and Society in holding a second series of Putney Debates, at St Mary's Church, Putney on 2–3 February, 370 years after the original debates took place there in 1647, was to scrutinize that issue and others that flow from it. While our concerns were provoked by the referendum of 2016 on whether to remain in the EU, the debate ranged more widely, bringing together a broad selection of citizens from diverse backgrounds to debate the constitutional challenges that confront us today. Over 500 people participated in those debates over the two days, marking a significant moment in our ongoing constitutional conversation. This short volume presents here for the first time the arguments voiced at the Putney Debates 2017, which can be watched again in full at www.fljs.org/ PutneyDebates2017-Videos.

I offer our contributors my warm thanks for taking up the invitation to develop their thoughts over the ensuing pages, and hope that this short volume goes some way toward addressing the call for better civic education, for the electorate and elected representatives alike, that rang out on more than one occasion over the course of those two days at St Mary's Church.

PART I

Parliament and the People

Popular Sovereignty vs Parliamentary Sovereignty

Sionaidh Douglas-Scott

I want to consider both popular and parliamentary sovereignty, and argue why neither is a complete solution to the quandaries Brexit poses for us.

Popular sovereignty is the belief that a state's legitimacy derives from the will of its people, who are the source of all political power. This idea is found in French revolutionary discourse, and it is 'We the People' who 'ordain and establish' the 1787 US Constitution, a reference invoked by Donald Trump when celebrating his inauguration as 'the day the people became the rulers of this nation again.'

Referendums are taken to be applications of popular sovereignty. Some argue that anything that frustrates the will of the people in a referendum is anti-democratic.

Who needs an Act of Parliament to trigger Article 50 when government has such a direct, powerful mandate?

What could be wrong with that claim? Quite a lot actually.

(1) History tells us that this theory of democracy – direct mandate from people to government – is often misused. In Latin America, plebiscites enabled tyrannical presidents to claim to embody the peoples' will over legislatures. And of course, Schmitt, that 'crown jurist of the Third Reich', posited a direct link between the people's will and the führer. That was democracy for him, as it was no doubt for Hitler and is today for other autocrats invoking rule of the people.

(2) In any case, it is clear that popular sovereignty is not the basis of the British Constitution. Nor are referendums. Their use countrywide only stems from 1975, and the most important issues, such as abolition of capital punishment or legalization of homosexuality, did not involve them.

Rather, *parliamentary* sovereignty has been the bedrock of the British Constitution, and UK politics is based on *representative* democracy. In 1653, Oliver Cromwell's *Instrument of Government* declared legislative power resided in the Lord Protector 'and the people', but this did not survive Cromwell. Even if we sometimes talk of 'sovereignty of the electorate', this only allows the people to choose a government, it does not ground the British Constitution in the authority of the people.

Maybe things should be different and we should embrace a written document said to derive its authority from 'the people'. But would this mean the June 2016 referendum result must be accepted as a mandate for the government, even for a hard Brexit? I do not think so. Many constitutions, even those expressed to derive their legitimacy from the people (such as the American and German Constitutions) do not provide for countrywide referendums at all. They also make it very difficult to amend their constitution – it is certainly not possible by bare majority of those voting, as in the EU referendum.

This is not to rule out referendums altogether, but to assert that the very idea of popular self-government must *presuppose* constitutional rules. There is no such thing as the objective 'general will' of the people. It is amorphous in nature, and in any case, we need laws to enable and implement it. A referendum in a constitutional democracy is always a product of law. Legal powers are needed to establish it and legal safeguards needed to interpret its constitutional significance.

(3) However, should popular sovereignty be argued as germane to Brexit, *Miller* and all that, consider this. Popular sovereignty *is* considered pertinent in Scotland, where it is claimed to date back to the 1320 Declaration of Arbroath. Might popular sovereignty form the basis of Scotland's own right to determine whether or not it exits the EU, given that 62 per cent of Scottish voters voted to remain? Surely it is the height of constitutional confusion if popular sovereignty is used to justify a Leave vote in England, where popular sovereignty is not part of the constitutional tradition, but ignored for Scotland, where it is?

Do these observations mean I am a keen enthusiast for parliamentary sovereignty? Does 'taking back control' mean a situation in which Westminster can do what it likes; override any human rights if it wishes? No, I do not think so.

But I do think the reasoning behind the key principle in *Miller* is compelling: government cannot change legislation, and especially not peoples' rights, by executive fiat. Parliament must have its say. This is Constitutional Law 101, and authorities supporting it date back to the Civil War. But accepting that does not mean unbridled parliamentary sovereignty. Perhaps the antidote to that is constitutional principle, which most countries have set in written constitutions to control major constitutional change. Without a codified or more substantive constitution, the UK lacks any such principles, and 'taking back control' may lead to its very opposite.

Electoral Reform
and the Constitution

David Runciman

The issue of electoral reform can often seem incidental to the deeper challenges facing our politics, at a time when there are so many other things to worry about: Brexit, the potential break-up of the UK and the looming presence across the water of President Trump. I do not believe that it is incidental. I want to argue that electoral reform remains an absolutely central issue. Indeed, the current electoral system is one of the root causes of the problems we face.

I do not make this case on the basis that first-past-the-post (FPTP) is inherently unfair, which is how electoral reformers often present it. Unfairness is a hard sell on this issue for three reasons. Firstly, complaints of unfairness tend to come from the losers under the current system – the Liberal Democrats, UKIP, the Green Party – which mean that they inevitably smack of sour grapes. Secondly, placing the premium on fairness means trying to come up with the fairest possible system, which is almost impossible, given the complexities involved. Every alternative proportional representation (PR) system has its flaws, making it all too easy to get bogged down in technicalities. Thirdly, if the basic issue is fairness, then I would agree there are more important things to worry about. The voting system is not the most unfair part of our society: economic inequalities, questions of gender and race, educational disadvantages all matter more.

My case against FPTP is not that it is unjust, but that it is dangerous. It produces a reckless, cavalier politics that panders to popular discontent rather than trying to channel and ameliorate it. Of course, that is what many of its supporters like about FPTP: it is immediately responsive to the public mood. At certain periods of relative stability that may be an advantage, to prevent democracy becoming excessively stale and managerial. But that is not the age we are currently living in. Our politics is increasingly unstable, and FPTP, by producing governments with the ability to act decisively rather than having to consult, is likely to make the instability worse.

FPTP is designed to create majorities in Parliament, even if no majority exists, rather than to represent majorities in the electorate at large. This mismatch is revealed by Brexit. The 52 per cent who voted to leave the EU are having their views represented by a government that speaks for only some of them; and the 48 per cent who voted to stay are having their views represented in Parliament by almost no one with any genuine authority at all. Because FPTP sees coalitions as a failure of the system rather than the default, there is little scope for governments that balance different perspectives. Labour is now waiting its turn under this system. When it next forms a government, it will have to square the circle of its pro-Remain and pro-Leave support. Having one party do two things at once is far more unstable than having two parties do one thing together.

Successive referendums – first in Scotland, then over the EU – are themselves symptomatic of the distortions of FPTP politics, which have encouraged the view that internal party differences are best resolved by a direct appeal to the people, rather than by parliamentary negotiation. Each vote adds to rather than resolving the divisions it is meant to address. Of course, FPTP is not the only system at work in Scotland. The Holyrood assembly has a hybrid PR system. The SNP are doing quite nicely under that as well. But it is worth remembering what a vote share of about 45 per cent means under the different systems: in the referendum, it meant a clear defeat; in Holyrood, it means something just shy of a majority; in Westminster, it means that the winner takes all.

I am not suggesting that if we were to move to a system of proportional representation it would be a panacea for our problems. Deep political divisions and popular discontent are clearly on the rise across the Western world, including in many European countries that operate with a form of PR. Nonetheless, it is striking that the two places where populism has emerged victorious are Britain and the US; so far, European electoral systems have served to temper rather than to unleash the worst of the anger. That may not last – but I would still rather the securities of PR than the insecurities of FPTP.

These are most visible in the US, where an antiquated electoral system produced an outcome that is a gross distortion of the true state of public opinion. Trump does not command majority support among the public yet his victory coincided with a victory for his party in both Houses of Congress. His inability to marshal the forces at his disposal may yet stymie his ambitions, but that is scant consolation. He is a populist given a power that far outmatches his popularity by an electoral system that fatally misrepresents the nature of his support.

It is not only governments that are corrupted by FPTP. Oppositions can be corrupted too, because it encourages them to cling on to the hope of outright victory even when it has become unrealistic. Even after its unexpected success in June 2017, Labour will struggle to win an overall majority. British politics looks split between two tribes who can't govern on their own and don't want to govern with anyone else. FPTP freezes political divisions in place, when what is needed is a form of politics that gets beyond them.

Electoral reform is not a sufficient condition of a better politics – there are many other things that also need to be addressed. But it is a necessary condition. Our current reliance on referendums, the entrenched partisan divisions in our politics, the grandstanding that is currently taking place over the future of the UK can all be traced back to an electoral system that produces distorted incentives and relatively unaccountable politicians acting on them.

Following Brexit, and then Trump, it was thought that a wave of populism would sweep the West, with Europe to follow suit; but it did not happen in the Netherlands, it has not happened in France and there are few signs of it happening in Germany. This despite the fact that those countries may face more acute challenges of cultural identity and economic instability than either the UK or the US. What makes the difference? It is hard to know for sure, but the boring old business of how electoral systems are designed to work is almost certainly a big part of it.

The Great Unanswered Question at Putney

John Rees

Leveller supporter Colonel Thomas Rainsborough uttered the most famous words that have come down to us from the Putney Debates of 1647. In the phrase now engraved in the balcony of St Mary's Church, Putney he said, 'For really I thinke that the poorest hee that is in England hath a life to live as the greatest he', and he continued, 'therefore truly, Sir, I thinke itt's cleare, that every man that is to live under a Government ought first by his owne consent to putt himself under that Government; and I doe thinke that the poorest man in England is nott att all bound in a strict sense to that government that he hath not had a voice to put himself under'.[1]

In reply to this outstandingly clear expression of democratic principles, his opponents in that debate, most notably Oliver Cromwell and his son-in-law Commissary General Henry Ireton, objected that if the poor were given the vote they would use it to take property away from the rich. Ireton proclaimed that his opposition to Rainsborough and the Levellers' *Agreement of the People* was because 'All the maine thinge I speake for is because I would have an eye to propertie ... lett every man consider with himself that hee doe nott goe that way to take away all propertie.'[2]

From that day to this the opposition between democracy and private property has been the axis around which much debate and many social, economic and political struggles have revolved. Over that time, we have learned some important things which neither Rainsborough nor Cromwell and Ireton could know.

Firstly, we know that parliamentary democracy is completely compatible with very great economic inequality and that it is far from obvious that if the poor have the vote they will attempt to take property from the rich.

Secondly, it is clear that on such occasions as the poor have chosen to use the vote to threaten the property of the rich, very considerable extra-parliamentary means have been deployed to stop them from doing so.

Therefore, the radically unanswered question of Putney is still very much alive. Indeed, it lies at the core of today's multifaceted political crisis of the British state.

Inequality in the UK is now at historically high levels.[3] There is a housing crisis greater than any since the 1930s. There is a crisis in health provision greater than at any time since the founding of the National Health Service. At work, people are now less well protected and less secure and are experiencing an historically unprecedented decline in real wages.

Put bluntly, no parent feels today as the parents of children growing up in the 1960s felt about the prospects for their children. They felt, and they were right, that their children would have a better education and better healthcare than they had; that they would have a better home and a better job. Now parents feel the exact opposite. They feel their children will find it harder and much more expensive to become well-educated and to remain healthy; that it will be much harder and much more expensive to find a home and a decently paid, secure job.

Nor is this phenomenon new. It has been building for more than a generation since the neoliberal, deregulation, privatizing economic model rose to dominance in the late 1970s and 1980s. But in the wake of the 2008 banking crash, a direct result of deregulated housing and banking sectors, it has built into a volcanic force capable of overthrowing long-established political patterns. In their very different ways, the rise of Bernie Sanders and Donald Trump in the US are both expressions of this underlying economic inequality. So are the crises in Greece and the watershed Brexit vote. So too is the rise of Jeremy Corbyn in the UK and of the French National Front. In short, long ignored economic inequality is producing political polarization.

Many analysts are tempted to imagine that because this problem manifested itself in political crises there must be a purely political solution. Candidates for what this might be vary: stay in or leave the EU, reform the voting system, establish a new constitution, break up or re-establish the UK.

No doubt many of these developments are desirable in their own right, while others are not. And some, no doubt, would be part of a comprehensive settlement of the crisis that now confronts us.

But all such solutions have a very pronounced tendency to ignore the Leveller in the room: they do not address the issue of economic inequality and what democracy means to those who are deprived of the fruits of their labour.

Anatole France long ago put his finger on the limits of merely formal political equality before the law: 'The law, in its majestic equality, forbids the rich as well as the poor to sleep under bridges, to beg in the streets, and to steal bread'.[4]

To move beyond formal political equality, we need to ask why it is so hard to imagine democracy in the economic field as well as the political field? Why not democratic control over jobs and pay, hours and conditions, investment and spending? Why is all this outside the competency of democracy? Why should the rich still be able to deny the poor the democratic means to decide how the wealth of a nation is used?

This is the question that the Putney Debates raised but which the Levellers, as small property owners themselves, could never fully answer. Leveller Richard Rumbold knew the issue when he said: 'No man comes into the world with a saddle on his back, neither any booted and spurred to ride him'.[5] Not a few would-be riders of their fellow creatures have been thrown by recent events. But we need more than the occasional fall from power to transform a system that is built on the interests of those who ride and not on the needs of those that carry them.

Notes

1 C.H. Firth, *The Clarke Papers: Selections from the Papers of William Clarke/Volumes I & II in One Volume* (Offices of the Royal Historical Society, 1992), pp. 300–1.

2 C.H. Firth, *The Clarke Papers: Selections from the Papers of William Clarke/Volumes I & II in One Volume* (Offices of the Royal Historical Society, 1992), pp. 301–2, 306.

3 As the Equality Trust, among many others, has shown. Available at: https://www.equalitytrust.org.uk/how-has-inequality-changed (accessed 19 April 2017).

4 A. France, *The Red Lily* (1894), Chapter 7. Available at: https://www.gutenberg.org/files/3922/3922-h/3922-h.htm (accessed 25 April 2017).

5 A. Southern, *Forlorn Hope: Soldier Radicals of the Seventeenth Century* (Lewes: The Book Guild, 2001), p. 147.

The Royal Prerogative, Referendums and the Outcomes of Brexit

Richard Sorabji

In the period of democracy in ancient Athens for most of the fifth century and some of the fourth, the adult male citizens eligible to vote were few beside the women, children, slaves and foreigners, like Aristotle. In one period they were herded by red-stained ropes to make them attend the democratic assembly. If they voted for war, it was they or their sons who would have to fight it. So they tended to know and be affected directly by their votes, and if they felt they had made a mistake, they could reverse their decision as soon as the next day. British society is far too big for all citizens to know, and be affected directly by political decision-making. Hence, in our representative democracy, decisions are taken by those who, through the electoral process, have shown (it is hoped) that they have the ability, and who have been given the authority to debate and insist on answers to the questions that confront the nation.

In 2017, the British Constitution worked well, when the executive (the Prime Minister and her chosen ministers) claimed that 'royal prerogative' gave them the power to decide whether to start the process of Brexit (Britain exiting the European Union [EU]). The Supreme Court, using powers of oversight affirmed in 1611, confirmed that it is for Parliament to decide, not the executive. But the new danger is that not only Parliament but also the electorate will be bypassed by the executive.

The electorate was asked to decide a question on which it could not know whom to believe: 'Should we be in or out of the European Union?' That question is now quite different from what it was when Britain first joined the Union. Then there had been years of negotiation, so that a great deal was known about the outcomes to be expected. Now very little is known at all. But the question the electorate could have answered, of what possible outcomes it would like or dislike, could not be decided by a referendum. Hence, the executive at present decides what outcomes it would like. But it should not claim that the electorate has endorsed them.

Electors could still be asked the neglected questions, even though exiting has been decided. Members of Parliament, parliamentary parties and reform groups still have time to ask them. What outcomes from exiting the EU would matter most to electors, and in what order of preference, and what items would they wish to add to an initial specimen list of outcomes to be achieved or avoided?

1. The control of borders against EU immigrants?
2. Do we need plausible results from initial trade discussions for making up trade lost with the EU?
3. Do we need to secure funding prospects, in the event of Brexit, for the National Health Service and concomitant home care, to release NHS beds?
4. Do we need to secure funding prospects for the new proposal to protect the so-called 'just about managing'?
5. Do we need to secure funding prospects for the new proposal to improve skills in the UK, to replace the need for immigrants?
6. Do we need to secure funding prospects for agriculture, in the event of Brexit?
7. Do we need freedom from judgments on human rights, or other matters, by the European Courts, or the right to appeal to those courts?

8. Do we need freedom from EU regulations – and if so, which? Should we retain EU regulations – and if so, which?

9. Do we need more secure jobs?

10. Do we need less inequality between rich and poor and the regeneration of derelict regions?

11. Should EU citizens working here in skilled jobs without fixed duration be allowed to stay?

12. Should citizens of EU countries who are immediate family members of British citizens be allowed to stay?

13. Should EU students selected on merit for British universities be allowed to come for the duration of their courses?

14. Should citizens of EU countries included in higher research projects located in, or funded by the UK, be allowed UK residence as needed by the project for the duration of their role in the project?

15. Does it matter whether Brexit enhances the sovereignty of the UK Parliament?

16. Are there any other desirable objectives?

These questions do not require technical knowledge about what outcomes Brexit might in fact plausibly achieve or prevent. Claims about the latter should be debated in Parliament by the people elected with the ability and authority to query such claims and demand answers. But Parliament was bypassed by the executive on this function too, since it was a previous prime minister who first announced that the electorate would be asked what decision to make in a referendum, which he wrongly treated as binding on Parliament. This naturally inhibited Parliament from carrying out its function, while also bypassing the appropriate questions to the electorate.

What Is This 'Populism'?

Akeel Bilgrami

A report in the *Financial Times* on President Trump's inaugural compared it to President Obama's first inaugural and declared: 'Obama radiated hope. Trump channelled rage'. This is factually correct. But if so, the fact needs diagnosis. Why hope then and rage now? An obvious answer is because the hope was not fulfilled, and so roughly half the electorate refused to believe that Obama's anointed successor in the Democratic Party – nor even the orthodox core of the Republican Party – would fulfil it either. Brexit seems to be channelling the same rage against Britain's political establishment. But the political establishment is not a self-standing class. Even a glance at the line-up of support for the Remain vote and for Hillary Clinton (both in the primaries against Bernie Sanders and in the presidential elections) shows the extent to which what underlies this political class is a parade of corporate and banking elites, ranging from the International Monetary Fund, Wall Street, the Organisation for Economic Co-operation and Development, and Soros, to the Governor of the Bank of England.

That leads us to the subject of how to understand the meaning of 'populism' as a term of opprobrium. The term is defined as 'ordinary people's opposition to elites'. So defined, it is too under-described to be a term of opprobrium. After all, *democracy* is intended to give ordinary people a chance to counter elites through representative politics. What populism today seems to add to democracy is that it also opposes the power of *un*elected officials with specific economic interests to dominate the formation of policies – with the general acquiescence of elected representatives.

But this still does not capture what we instinctively recoil from in populism. How can it be wrong to oppose the voluntary implicit surrender of sovereignty by elected law- and policymakers to unelected wielders of elite financial interests?

Suppose, then, for a moment, that a working or workless person in Nottingham or Crete or Seville were to ponder the humane policies that some nations in

Europe came to embrace since the Second World War; policies which provided safety nets (whether of health or education or housing) for people like him. He might ask: What was the site where these safety nets were administered and implemented? And he would answer: Well, the site of the nation. He might scratch his head and wonder: Has there ever been a supranational site at which welfare was ever administered? What would a mechanism that dispensed it at a supranational site even so much as look like?

Now, of course, such a person might go on beyond these shrewd questions to associate supranational affiliation with immigrant hordes who not only deprive him of economic opportunities, but dilute the centuries long national culture of which he is so proud. But there is no logical link between those excellent former questions and these latter trumped up anxieties. One may rightly ask the questions without having these anxieties. And so here at last we have what is the defining element of populism from which we recoil. The term stands for precisely the assumption of such a link, a link that is uncompulsory.

So a question arises: Whence the compulsion to make this *un*compulsory link? And here we must resist the temptation to blame the people themselves. The assumption they make of such a link is not due to their feebleness of mind but to a wide variety of distortions not only by the media they read and watch, but by the political class, and not just the extreme elements of that class but the political establishment. We cannot forget that the British Prime Minister's Remain campaign ratcheted up the immigration theme to prevent its being owned by his more extreme Right opposition, just as Obama in his first campaign was far worse on immigration than John McCain, again with a view to gaining ownership of a Republican platform, for electoral gains.

So the lesson is this. Even if we identify what we recoil from in populism as the uncompulsory linking of sound questions with unsound anxieties, this cannot simply be attributed to an *intrinsic incapacity* in the judgement of ordinary people, but must be attributed to the failure of public education provided by the media and the political class. One cannot believe in democracy and dismiss the electorate as vile or stupid. For the electorate is shaped by what *knowledge* it possesses.

For twenty hundred years, philosophers have said that the central ethical question is: What ought we to do? But in our own complex time, the more crucial prior question has become: What ought we to know?

On 'Popular Sovereignty'

Vernon Bogdanor

Those who opposed our membership of the EU sought to restore parliamentary sovereignty. But their success has meant that parliamentary sovereignty is being trumped by popular sovereignty. Parliament is now constrained not by Brussels, but by the people.

Theresa May has said that, although the referendum was advisory, the government regards itself as bound by the result; and MPs will almost certainly feel bound by it as well. MPs, therefore, are, for the first time in our parliamentary history, required to vote for a policy which most of them oppose. That is an event without precedent in our long parliamentary history.

The referendum shows how out of touch the House of Commons is with public opinion. Around 75 per cent of MPs were for Remain. So were the leaders of the three major parties. Only two parties with a combined total of nine out of 650 MPs were for Brexit – UKIP with one MP and the Democratic Unionist Party of Northern Ireland with eight.

The referendum was a striking exercise in democratic participation in which 72 per cent voted, the highest turnout in any national election or referendum since 1992. In general elections, around three-quarters of the seats are safe for one party. But, in the referendum, every vote counted and there was no equivalent to the safe seat. There was therefore an incentive for all to vote, and a particular incentive perhaps for Labour voters living in safe seats in the north, many of whom seem not to have voted since the time of Margaret Thatcher. Turnout was highest in the Leave areas and lowest in the Remain areas – Scotland, Northern Ireland, London and among the young – the very groups most vocal in calling for a second referendum!

Some Remainers have criticized the outcome as inappropriate for a multinational state since the Scots and Northern Irish are being forced out of the EU even though they voted to Remain. One wonders if this criticism would have gained so much traction had a narrow majority in England for Leave been overcome by majorities in Scotland and Northern Ireland for Remain.

However, the notion of popular sovereignty has come under attack from those who do not like the outcome. Their criticisms were prefigured by M. Jean Rey, the former President of the European Commission, when, in London, on 17 July 1974, he spoke out against the referendum being proposed by Harold Wilson's government. 'A referendum on this matter', M. Rey said, 'consists of consulting people who don't know the problems instead of consulting people who know them. I would deplore a situation in which the policy of this great country should be left to housewives. It should be decided instead by trained and informed people'. Some on the liberal left now oppose popular sovereignty, deploying the arguments used by conservatives in the nineteenth century against the expansion of the franchise – that the people are too ignorant and confused to know their own interests, too easily misled by deceitful propaganda and that their interests are best represented by those with property and education.

The exercise of popular sovereignty has, as Theresa May pointed out, revealed deep fissures in British society between those who have done well out of globalization, the exam-passing classes, and those who have not. The liberal left has tended to ignore the latter group, which is not easy to accommodate within its framework of identity politics. The politics of identity concerns itself primarily with the identity of minorities – whether subnational, ethnic or sexual – not the identity of the white English working class. Indeed, any expression of that identity has been seen as somehow illegitimate or even racist; and, since the referendum, there has been much criticism of the supposed bigotry of Leave voters.

But, if one seeks to discover bigotry in Britain, one has to look elsewhere – to the universities, for example, including, sadly, Oxford, my old university, where Alex Chalmers, the non-Jewish Chair of the University Labour Club, recently resigned from his position, saying that 'a large proportion' of its members 'had problems with Jews'. On the left of the Labour Party, if non-Jewish MPs such as Jess Phillips are to be believed, anti-Semitism is combined with misogyny. She told *The Times* last September that, 'there's misogyny at the top' of the party. Having had 600 rape threats in a single night, she has reported the worst of the trolls to her party but had heard nothing back. She has received 'hundreds and hundreds of pages of abuse' with 'an anti-Semitic undercurrent', feels that there is definitely anti-Semitism in the party and that Corbyn needs to clamp down on it. So far he has not done so. I somehow doubt that anti-Semitism and rape threats are quite such a problem among those who exercised their democratic rights in the referendum.

In Britain, therefore, the danger of bigotry arises not from the exercise of popular sovereignty or 'populism', but from the intolerance of elites – many of them university-educated. The vote for Brexit was in part an assertion of English identity, and the referendum shows the growing importance of the English question. But that question is at bottom a cultural and social, not a constitutional one.

Building a New Social Commons: People and Parliament Working Together

Anna Coote

I am going to focus on the commons – not the House of Commons but the 'commons'. There is a growing 'commoning' movement, in Europe and across the world where people are claiming shared control of resources that are central to human life, like water, land, energy. Groups organize to manage and distribute these resources in the interests of everyone, not just the rich and powerful.

Protagonists of the commons are challenging the 'enclosure' of life's necessities by powerful corporate interests, often supported by government. They recognize that everyone has a right to these necessities and we all share responsibility for making sure everyone's rights are respected.

These rights exist only if they are claimed, fought for and defended. So the commons is a process – a political struggle – as well as the resources that are struggled for.

And just as we need natural resources, like land and water, so we need social resources – help from others to stay well and lead good lives. That is why we must claim and build a new social commons. Protection from risks we cannot cope with alone – ill health, homelessness, frailty, unemployment. Access to education, social care and a decent income. Not as concessions, but as a matter of right for all.

This means reimagining and reinventing the best elements of the welfare state. To embody the collective ideal, to put people in control, to assert and defend the principle of fair and equal access.

It is urgent to do this now. To find new language and ways of working that will strengthen solidarity and social justice at a time when politics are increasingly divisive and exclusionary, and to help us withstand the shock of leaving the EU.

The founding values and purpose of the postwar settlement have been worn to shreds by the application of market rules – contracting out, competition and choice, privatization – and by spending cuts that have left a tattered, tawdry safety net.

It is no surprise that people feel angry and cheated. But if there is a growing urge to throw out the bathwater of established institutions, we must rescue the baby of collective action, shared resources and mutual aid. (The EU, whatever its flaws, has been a source and defence of progressive social policies.)

The New Economics Foundation has proposals for building the social commons, which I have no time to summarize here. Just two points.

Firstly, the commoning movement is not about 'rolling back the state' but transforming relations between people and the state. It is a fight against the enclosure of power, which is also one of life's necessities. For the social commons, there is a crucial role for a transformed state, in setting standards, distributing funds and guaranteeing fair access.

Secondly, the social commons must be shaped through democratic dialogue. We have good formats for involving people in decisions – town hall meetings, digital forums, citizens' juries, people's assemblies. At best, they tap into the wisdom that people form in their everyday lives and enable them to engage in informed discussion, scrutinizing evidence, questioning experts, arguing and debating and changing their minds.

This is a far cry from the referendum format, where powerful interests set out to enclose the popular vote.

But policymakers too easily brush off decisions formed through democratic dialogue. So the challenge is how to create a three-way dynamic – between popular participation, formal expertise and representative politics. With national parliaments and local councils as active champions and participants – rather than bystanders or manipulative sponsors – in a national deliberative dialogue. That is how we want to start building the social commons.

So, in conclusion, let us imagine a future where our ways of doing politics are focused on the commons. The means of securing life's necessities – natural, social and political – for everyone. Shared resources equally accessible according to need, enshrined in laws forged through open, informed, democratic dialogue. And an end to the enclosures of the twenty-first century.

Brexit and the Case for a People's Constitution

Alexandra Runswick

The seemingly innocuous phrasing of Article 50, that it must be 'triggered according to the member state's own constitutional arrangements', created a legal and political crisis. Parliamentary sovereignty, long argued to be the cornerstone of our democracy, was challenged by the popular sovereignty of the referendum result.

As we leave the EU, the UK's unwritten constitution will come under increasing strain as we redefine our position in the world, and with a once-in-a-generation opportunity to take back real control, now is time for a people's constitution. By this I mean a single codified document which sets out what the government can and cannot do in our name, drafted after public involvement in a deliberative process to determine what we the people think should be in a constitution.

For me, these two strands are equally important – a codified constitution could be drafted by eminent lawyers and academics. But unless we collectively help to shape the principles, rights and freedoms in the constitution, it will do very little to address the very real disconnect between Parliament and the people.

It will simply reinforce that politics is something that is done to people and a democracy is somewhere we live rather than something we actively participate in.

As events in the US have shown, constitutions only work when people are willing to fight to uphold them, where judges are willing to tell an executive that they do not have the power to do something, where Acting Attorney Generals are willing to refuse to implement executive orders they do not believe are lawful.

For that to happen I believe we in the UK need our 'We the People' moment.

It is often said that codifying our constitution would go against our tradition of incremental reform.

Now, whatever confidence the current government has in their plans, it is undoubtable that we are embarking on a course that is without precedent and is anything but incremental.

That is why I think we have an opportunity to strengthen our democracy.

One of the challenges we face in our democracy is that there is very little space for public deliberation. We tend to focus on the formal institutions of our democracy but not how we build and strengthen our democratic culture. A deliberative process in which we came together to discuss what we think should be protected in a constitution would be an important step in rebuilding our democratic culture and giving people a sense of ownership.

The government's battle in the courts to withdraw the UK from the EU using the royal prerogative highlighted the fact that the lack of a codified constitution leaves our democracy, and many of the important mechanisms that underpin it, open to interpretation by the government of the day.

From grey areas around the legal force of referendums through to the limits of prerogative powers, our unwritten constitutional conventions, where they exist at all, have more often than not been a source of confusion rather than clarity. As we move through the process of leaving the EU, these fundamental constitutional questions will only become more pressing, even critical to the survival of the Union.

A long-term settlement is needed, and a written constitution, devised by and for the people, can deliver the certainty we need in our own democratic system to reshape our position in the world. To 'face the future together', as the Prime Minister set out, we must shape the future together.

There must be a clear, consistent and scrutinizable balance between national interest, the interest of the government of the day, and the rights and freedoms of citizens, and we need a new constitutional settlement to resolve three broad questions.

(1) We need clarity about where power lies, what powers the devolved parliaments have, how they relate to each other and who has the authority to make changes to the relationship. While powers continue to be devolved, these more fundamental questions have never been resolved.

Rather, there have been conventions and understandings, many of which the Supreme Court's judgment called into question.

Setting out where power lies also means being clear about the separation of powers – the different powers of the executive (the government and civil service), the legislature, Parliament (which makes laws but does not administer them) and the judiciary (which rules on what is lawful when this is disputed).

(2) A written constitution would also define what rights and powers we the people have. It would not only set out key rights, from freedom of speech to privacy, but also rights of assembly of voting and standing in elections. It could go further than the traditional political and civil rights often incorporated into written constitutions around the world. It could, for example, include social and economic rights such as the rights to housing and healthcare, as the South African Constitution does. Crucially, it would also set out how these rights are protected and what we could do if the government breached these rights.

(3) Most importantly, a written constitution would set out what the government can and cannot do in our name, rather than allowing it to act in whatever way it pleases, until challenged in the courts. It would be a sad irony that if, after a campaign centred around 'taking back control', more power were to be ceded to Westminster and the political establishment rather than to the people. It would be a betrayal of voters whose trust in politics is waning, contrary to the very spirit and aims of the Leave campaign, and a lost opportunity to empower the people of the UK.

PART II

Changing and Strengthening
the Role of the People

Is Representative Democracy Ripe for Review and Modification in Favour of More Direct Democracy?

Philip Kay

In 1953, Professor Richard Pares observed about eighteenth-century England that: 'In a mixed constitution, where the bounds of the respective powers are not precisely and effectively fixed, their actual relations at any time will be determined by the accident of personalities on the one hand and, on the other, by the advantage which the need of surmounting emergencies ... may give to one institution or another'.[1]

It is precisely such accidents and advantages that have led us, over the last 40 years or so, toward a more direct form of democracy in the shape of the referendum.

As that old fox Harold Wilson figured out in 1975, a referendum can be a way of surmounting an emergency in one's own party. David Cameron thought he could do the same and catastrophically failed.

Referendums have had, of course, only a short history in the UK, perhaps because politicians as diverse as Clement Attlee and Margaret Thatcher regarded them as 'a device of dictators and demagogues' – a view with which one might have some sympathy when one hears phrases such as 'the will of the people' and 'the people have spoken' being bandied about in the wake of a narrow vote in a non-binding EU referendum. There have in fact ever been only three UK-wide referendums, two about our involvement with Europe and one in 2011 about the alternative vote (AV) method. Devolution, sovereignty and independence have put in cameo appearances in various regional referendums, but war (which, by the way, was the main issue on which the popular assemblies in Republican Rome voted) has never made it onto the playlist of our national referendums. Perhaps war is too serious a matter to be left to Joe Public. But, one might argue, technology does now give us the ability to vote in referendums, frequently and remotely, via smartphones and laptops. So should we have more referendums? Should we vote for war on an iPhone app?

The trouble is that the political discourse surrounding a popular vote on a single issue will inevitably simplify and distort sometimes extraordinarily complex matters. During last year's EU campaign, facts were elastic concepts. Ahead of the vote, the Radio 4 programme *More or Less* ran a two-hour analysis of the statistics being cited by both sides. The overwhelming majority were just plain wrong. But the result of the referendum was a vote in favour of a high-risk gamble with completely unpredictable consequences.

For all its faults, thorough debate in Parliament allows our leaders to be challenged and their statements to be scrutinized; but that is not to deny that representative democracy is ripe for review. The day before the referendum, a BBC poll showed that about 75 per cent of our 650 MPs supported remain. But our parliamentary system magnified the 52 per cent popular vote for Leave to something closer to 61 per cent, on a constituency basis. So about 365 of those original 479 Remainers supported the government's EU motion, the so-called 'Brexit Bill'. And there is the rub. Maybe I am in a naive minority of one, but I voted for my representative in Parliament because, while I did not agree with every one of her cocktail of views, I did with those that I believed to be important, including, in my case, remaining in the EU.

Last night she voted to leave. Next time round, I can try and vote her out, but I would have preferred her to have been one of those 47 Labour MPs who last night voted according to their own judgement or conscience. That is what I elected her to do.

So in summary, I am not a fan of referendums, but our representatives need to adjust their behaviour or they will lose the small amount of credibility they have left.

Note

1 R. Pares, *King George III and the Politicians* (Oxford: Oxford University Press, 1953), p. 61.

'The People is my Cæsar': Jeremy Bentham's Radical Democratic State

Philip Schofield

Jeremy Bentham (1748–1832), the philosopher and reformer, was the founder of classical utilitarianism, the doctrine that an action is right to the extent that it promotes the greatest happiness or well-being of those affected. In his *Constitutional Code*, he drew up a blueprint for a radical, democratic, republican state. He wrote: 'Sovereignty is in *the people*.'[1] Constitutional Code gave institutional structure to Bentham's pronouncement that, 'The people is my Cæsar.'[2]

Bentham recognized that there existed a natural opposition of interests between rulers and subjects. Rulers, no different from everyone else in being predominantly self-interested, would strive to promote their own interest or well-being, no matter the consequences for the community as a whole, and, given that they possessed power and influence, would succeed. The key figure was 'the chief executive functionary' – the monarch in a monarchy, the president in a republic – who would use their power, wealth and influence to corrupt members of the legislature, for instance, through the award of honours, contracts or lucrative employments.

The only political system in which this 'sinister sacrifice' could be avoided was a representative democracy, since it was only there that effective arrangements could be put in place – 'securities against misrule' – to replace the opposition of interests between rulers and subjects with an identification of interests. The purpose of constitutional law was to render it impossible for rulers to promote their own interest without thereby promoting the interest of the community as a whole.[3]

What were the main institutional features of Bentham's democratic state? The electorate, consisting of the sovereign people, would be characterized by universal suffrage, subject to a literacy test; equal electoral districts; the secret ballot; and annual elections. A single chamber legislature would be 'omnicompetent', that is, there would be no unchangeable or 'entrenched' laws, since to make such laws was to lay claim to infallibility, and no one was infallible. With annual elections, together with the power of constituents to remove their deputy at any time by means of petition and majority vote, the legislature would not lose touch with the people. Nor would there be any need for referendums.

The executive, headed by a prime minister, would be subject to the control of the legislature, as would the judiciary, headed by a justice minister. Bentham rejected the standard notion of the separation of powers. Instead of each branch of government having its independent sphere, there would be lines of subordination – the executive and judiciary would be subordinate to the legislature, and the legislature subordinate to the people.

This essay's title, I must confess, is a partial quote. In full, Bentham stated: 'The people is my Cæsar: I appeal from the present Cæsar to Cæsar better informed.' A democratic structure of government was not enough. Within that structure, there needed to be further 'securities against misrule': for instance, there should be no titles of honour and no religious establishment (for Bentham, theology had as much place in a law book as expletives in a cookery book);[4] that officials, including the prime minister and other ministers, should have passed relevant examinations (the executive would in effect be part of the civil service); and, very importantly, all government actions should be done openly and be publicly recorded, unless a case had been made for secrecy. If the people were to ensure that the interest of the community was promoted by government, they needed to know what government was doing, and who precisely was doing it.

I have outlined some elements of Bentham's radical democratic state. But how relevant is Bentham today? Judith Resnik, the Yale legal scholar, has argued that we should go back to Bentham in thinking about the legal system, and his plea that justice be accessible, the law cognoscible;[5] Jon Elster, the political scientist, in thinking about decision-making in our legal and political systems;[6] and Richard Layard, the social scientist, in placing the promotion of happiness at the centre of our policy initiatives.[7] Given that Bentham gave systematic form to the democratic ideas advanced in St Mary's Church, Putney, three and a half centuries ago, and provided the rationale for the People's Charter of 1848, perhaps we should go back to Bentham in thinking about democracy.

Notes

1 Jeremy Bentham, *The Collected Works of Jeremy Bentham: Constitutional Code: Vol. I.*, ed. F. Rosen and J.H. Burns (Oxford: Clarendon Press, 1983), p. 25.

2 *The Works of Jeremy Bentham*, ed. John Bowring, 11 vols (Edinburgh: William Tait, 1838–43), x. 73.

3 Jeremy Bentham, *First Principles Preparatory to Constitutional Code*, ed. P. Schofield (Oxford: Clarendon Press, 1989), pp. 229–331.

4 Jeremy Bentham, *Preparatory Principles*, ed. D.G. Long and P. Schofield (Oxford: Clarendon Press, 2016), pp. 167–8.

5 Judith Resnik, 'Bring Back Bentham: "Open Courts," "Terror Trials," and Public Spheres', *Law & Ethics of Human Rights* V(1) (2011), Article 1.

6 Jon Elster, *Securities Against Misrule: Juries, Assemblies, Elections* (Cambridge: Cambridge University Press, 2013).

7 Richard Layard, 'This is the Greatest Good', *Guardian*, 14 September 2009, p. 32.

We Need Fewer Referendums, with Higher Thresholds

Robert Hazell

I am going to address the question of the place of the referendum in our constitution. It asks whether the referendum should become a permanent device; if so, whether referendums should be binding or advisory; whether special majorities should be required; how to make sure people are well informed about the issues, and know the consequences. I am not going to give definitive answers to these questions, because as I shall explain, we are trying to establish a Commission to look into precisely these issues, and I do not want to pre-empt their task; but I shall set out the agenda for the Commission, and suggest some possible answers.

To the first question, referendums are now an established part of our democracy, and there is no going back. We cannot deny a second independence referendum in Scotland if that is what the Scottish government and people want. For over 40 years we have said to the people of Northern Ireland that they have a standing right to hold a referendum on whether to reunite with the South, in a border poll. At a minimum, a referendum is recognized as necessary for any part of the UK to secede. What we have offered to Scotland and Northern Ireland, we cannot deny to other parts of the UK.

So we cannot exclude referendums from our political system, but we can think hard about what their place should be, and how they should be run, in the light in particular of our three most recent referendums: on the voting system in 2011, Scottish independence in 2014 and EU membership in 2016. Current concern focuses mainly on the EU referendum, but we should not forget that the quality of debate in the alternative vote (AV) referendum was just as bad, and that the Scottish independence referendum would have been almost as much a leap in the dark, if Scotland had voted Yes, as the EU referendum. Alex Salmond's White Paper was a wish list dependent on the decisions of others, in particular the UK government and the EU, in much the same way that Theresa May's White Paper will be a wish list dependent on the response of the other 27 member states.

For the last six months, I have been working to establish an independent Commission into the role and conduct of referendums, to consider the role of referendums in British politics, and how the rules and practice can be improved. It would be a successor to the Constitution Unit's 1996 Commission on the Conduct of Referendums, chaired by Sir Patrick Nairne, which led to the first statutory regulation of referendums in the Political Parties, Elections and Referendums Act 2000, the Act which created the Electoral Commission. Our new Commission will be informed by comparative study of the conduct and regulation of referendums in other mature democracies, and if we can raise the funding, its ideas will be tested through three citizens' assemblies, groups of randomly selected citizens meeting for a whole weekend in different parts of the UK, to ensure the Commission is more than just an elite affair.

The Commission's proposed terms of reference will cover:

- the appropriate place of referendums in UK contemporary democracy;
- the provision of public information, and promotion of informed debate;
- the regulation of the designated campaign groups;
- the role of government during the campaign;

- the legal effect of referendums, and whether any supermajority should be required.

In the interest of brevity, I will focus on the last, thresholds and supermajorities. These tend to be thought of in simple arithmetical terms, a requirement that the threshold should be higher than a simple majority of those voting, 50 per cent plus one. But there is a whole range of options for increasing the threshold:

- There could be a minimum turnout requirement, as, in effect, there was for the 1979 referendum in Scotland.
- There could be a federal requirement, of the kind found in Australia and Canada, that a referendum must be supported by a minimum number of states or provinces; or in the UK, a minimum number of the four nations.
- There could be a requirement of a second referendum once the terms of the new settlement are known. We recommended that in a book we wrote about Scottish independence in 2002, and proposals for a second referendum on the negotiated terms have resurfaced in connection with our departure from the EU.

I hope to have said enough about the Commission's role and tasks. Now is the time to start the public discussion of the terms on which we want referendums to be conducted, before we are confronted with the next one.

Referendums for EU Politics?

Anne Deighton

The question of whether referendums are the appropriate tool to resolve complex issues is a difficult one, and here I will focus on the place of referendums in British politics as they relate to the EU. I will make three key points that contribute to our debate.

(1) The first concerns the referendum as a tool of politics. In the UK, the referendum has an uncomfortable place in the complicated jigsaw of our constitution. It has been used only twice in relation to EC/EU politics (and only infrequently in domestic politics), and this alone makes it difficult to consider it as anything other than either a novelty, or an anomaly. In both 1975 and 2016, the referendum was advisory, although in practice, each referendum result (Stay in 1975;

Leave in 2016) was considered definitive, at least in the short term.

The political party in power at the time: Labour in 1975, and the Conservatives in 2016, opted for a referendum in the context of bitterly divisive internal party politics. Labour was split on ideological grounds – seeing the EC as 'a capitalist club'. In 2016, the Conservatives felt electorally threatened by the rise of UKIP and sought survival through greater self-reliance (national sovereignty) in international and domestic affairs. In both cases, at the highest echelons, there was open and public party disagreement on the EC/EU. This reduced the capacity for either party to secure the support of their party faithful.

Party politics has also muddied the relationship between the sovereignty of Parliament in relation to the 2016 referendum result. The constitutional difficulties on parliamentary versus prerogative rights to set in train the decision to leave the EU were expertly exposed by the Supreme Court. What UK referendums over the EC/EU have done is to expose the inability of the British party system to come to an accommodation with the aims and working practices of European integration. Europe has always been a cross-cutting issue for the major British parties. In this sense, the UK has always been an outlier in the Continental European integration process and the new kind of domestic and international politics that it promised.

The referendum has also been an uncomfortable tool in the sense that, while it apparently gives voters a direct and influential 'say', the practical structuring of the referendums (without equal financing in 1975) and exclusion of 16-year-olds from the vote in 2016 (although they could in the Scottish independence referendum of 2014) were both amateurish and unfair. Further, the wording of the question itself has been oversimplified and the consequences of a vote either way was not made clear. This has led to obfuscation (practised to a disgraceful extent by both sides in 2016) about consequences, and thus reinforced the phenomenon that the referendum was, like many local government and European Parliament elections, a second-order matter. Voters expressed opinions that were not directly related to the question asked. (Giving elites 'a good kicking' is one fine example of this, not least as the elites most consistently under fire in the years running up to the referendum were national MPs and peers themselves – the anticipated holders of post-Brexit parliamentary sovereignty).

(2) The referendum experience in the EC/EU has been very different. The UK did not have a referendum in 1972 before accession in January 1973. The Danes (Yes), Irish

(Yes) and Norwegians (No) did have referendums before finally joining. Indeed, France held a referendum as well, to gauge whether the French wanted the 1972 enlargement to go ahead (Yes). Referendums before enlargement have become a pattern in the EU, along with referendums on treaty changes over time. Some of these referendums have also been striking in their impact – especially the defeat of the Constitutional Treaty proposal in 2005 (when UK Prime Minister Tony Blair had also considered a referendum until the treaty was buried by the referendums in France and the Netherlands).

The difference with these referendums is that the proposals have been more specific, and the public better informed about the consequences of their vote. Furthermore, if an issue is turned down, it has been modified and then taken back to the electorate. Nevertheless, the referendum, it seems to me, remains a fickle tool for change – at root it exposes the limitations of MPs at the national and the European Parliament level. It should be noted both that, in some European constitutions, the referendum is a part of the constitutional apparatus, which is quite different from the UK constitutional framework. Maybe new technologies may in time change the referendum effectiveness and landscape in the longer term.

(3) All this leaves the British government with an enormous political and diplomatic challenge (some say 'disaster' or 'train crash'), a challenge that may in the end prove to be beyond its capacity. This is not least because it has had to find its negotiating red lines by on-the-job improvisation (no European Court of Justice, control of immigration) and within the greater context of the EU's own rules (on the Single European Market in particular), because of the woolly and inept British referendum process. It should be noted that the historical experience of the British doing trade negotiations with the European Economic Community in the 1950s is also alarming – as we reached our Plan G (from Plan A to G) to create a free trade area, only to have this vetoed – since the sense within the European Commission was that the UK was trying to wreck the whole integration project by diluting it from the outside. Post-referendum negotiators, read your history books!

In the interim, the way in which voting was counted has exposed the divisions between English and Scottish/ Northern Irish voters which may deliver unintended consequences of a very great magnitude. This challenges the value of head-counting politics on a non-nationwide basis.

The government has rejected the capacity of the British Parliament to decide on any eventual deal.

The constitutional implications of this are enormous, and counter-intuitive to a democrat. The irony is that, having set out on the referendum path in 1975 in a way that has been ad hoc, if not slap-happy, it may be that only another referendum can trump that of 2016. There should therefore be another referendum – difficult and technical as it may be – to square the constitutional circle in two years or thereabouts.

If we do leave after 2019, we will never get a deal that is any better than that which we now have. So there will surely be a reapplication and then referendum when, a couple of decades down the line – if the EU still exists – we find that there is no alternative, and find ourselves in the line to renew our membership.

Social Media and Democracy

Linda Risso

In assessing the health of our democracy, I will focus on the positive contribution that social media makes to the democratic process and how it can be a source of empowerment as well as a source of knowledge.

There are of course concerns about social media. We know that it can lead to the polarization of society, become a tool for abuse, and spread misinformation and fake news. There are alarming claims that social media is damaging or at the very least transforming the nature of Western democracy. It is undeniable that the phenomenon has a strong and far-reaching impact on the political debate as well as on society more broadly.

Yet it is important to remind ourselves of the immense opportunities afforded by social media in terms of empowering citizens and civil society, of mobilizing public opinion and of allowing often marginalized sectors of the public to become involved in the democratic process.

I will start with three key points that make social media widespread and powerful.

One is 'space': social media, particularly when linked to mobile technologies, allows us to communicate in real time with experts, political leaders, activists, as well as family and friends across the world, at any time. We can connect with people with whom we share interests and concerns. We can be informed about new laws and schemes that have direct impact on our lives. We can learn about topics close to our interests, jobs and livelihoods.

Because of its very nature, social media allow the mobilization of sectors of society across borders. The Women's Marches that took place the day after President Trump's inauguration ceremony are a powerful example of coordination across the globe thanks to social media.

Today, social media and mobile technology penetrate geographical areas that had previously been left behind by scientific and technological change. Around 46 per cent of the world population, equivalent to roughly 3.6 billion people, has an internet connection today. In 1995, it was less than 1 per cent.[1] The rate of growth is astonishing, and it is having a dramatic impact on the world economy, society and democracy.

The second point is a marked change in the distribution of power and knowledge in the sphere of social media. We now have new, less constrained platforms where dialogue takes place. News corporations, big businesses and government are part of the discussion, but they are no longer the sole initiators. They have become one of many interlocutors with equal, and often disputed, authority.

Today, it is quite common for news corporations to rely on information and evidence sent by citizens or by witnesses to a particular event. The new phenomenon of 'citizen journalists' is increasingly widespread, and comes with a complex series of practical and ethical conundrums.

The third element concerns the cost of mass communication. These have come down dramatically, for information creation and circulation, as well as for participation. Owning a telephone and having access to the internet is now open to a large sector of the public. According to the Office for National Statistics, in 2016, 82 per cent of adults (41.8 million) in Great Britain used the internet daily or almost daily, compared 35 per cent (16.2 million) in 2006. Crucially, in 2016, 70 per cent of adults accessed the internet 'on the go' using a mobile phone or smartphone, nearly double the 2011 estimate of 36 per cent.[2] Circulating a piece of research, a news item or an official report now takes only a few seconds at virtually no cost.

What does this mean in practice and what does it say about the changing nature of democracy?

Social media enable governments and politicians to be in touch with their voters, to speak to groups of individuals – even on a one-to-one basis – in a way and with an immediacy that was previously inconceivable. At the opposite end, constituents can express their views directly to their MP, from the comfort of their home. They can read Select Committees' reports, follow the work of Parliament and send queries to ministers and leading government figures.

A new global awareness is also emerging among the public. The international campaign to abolish nuclear weapons (ICAN) that culminated in a historic UN Security Council decision to start formal discussions in 2017 is a good example of this new global awareness and political activism. The ICAN campaign relied heavily on social media to mobilize support in several UN countries and to put pressure on national governments.[3]

Crucially, social media can potentially give a voice to the most vulnerable and marginalized members of our society. I am referring in particular to the elderly. Mobile technologies and social media can break the barrier of isolation and can allow elderly members of society to feel more connected with the rest of society. They can gain easier access to medical advice and be part of support networks within their own community. Yet, according to the Office for National Statistics, 'nearly half of single pensioners still have no internet access at all'.[4] For this reason, there is a strong argument in favour of embracing mobile technologies and social media and of making sure that they are as widespread as possible.

It is also worth mentioning briefly here the life-saving role that social media can play during crises and emergencies. Many young people survived the Utoya massacre in Norway by sharing information about the movements of Anders Breivik during the attack on the island. More recently, victims trapped under the ruins of the Italian earthquake were saved thanks to social media and the triangulation of mobile phone GPS signals.

Social media also shapes the creation and circulation of knowledge and expertise. Like politicians, experts too are now within much easier reach. This is an important phenomenon, particularly if we consider, for example, the circulation of scientific information, legal expertise and medical advice.

The role of experts is changing and many engage proactively and reach out to the wider public. They help us to understand the complexities and ramifications of key issues. A good example is the Article 50 legal challenge at the High Court and at the Supreme Court. Lawyers like Schona Jolly, David Allen Green and Jo Maugham took it upon themselves to make the rather technical discussions as accessible as possible. They tweeted during the court hearings, commented on the key terms and explained the content of the courts' decisions in simple and accessible messages. They redirected users to articles, blogs and publications where further details could be found. Through social media, they made an otherwise complex issue interesting and even compelling. Other experts and academics have picked up on it and in recent months there has been a flurry of articles on Henry VIII, the royal prerogative, and the *Attorney-General v De Keyser's Royal Hotel* case in 1920 which considered the principles on which the courts decide whether statute has fettered prerogative power.

One point that is rarely mentioned but that is crucial in examining how social media shapes our democracy and our information environment are the algorithms at work behind the scenes. Algorithms are the DNA code of the internet. They are the reason why some items appear at the top of our internet searches, what bits of news and comments we see first and what people we contact via social media. There is clear evidence that algorithms are designed in a way that makes us read things with which we already agree and connect with people with whom we already share views. Algorithms create bubbles in which people with the same ideas tend to talk to one another, often unaware of different perspectives. The Chancellor of Germany Angela Merkel was right when, in October 2016, she spoke about the need for search engines and social media companies to be more transparent about their algorithms and to work with governments to prevent polarization of society, radicalization and the spread of misinformation and fake news.[5]

Despite the potential of social media to empower citizens and connect all members of society, it is undeniable that its use is not without risk. The sheer cacophony of opinions, data, facts and counterfacts can be confusing and misleading. I do not want to discuss here the issue of deliberate abuse of social media and what is now known as 'fake news'. This implies a willing manipulation of the information environment through the circulation of false information to create confusion and foster relativism. Evidence is also mounting about the use of social media by data companies for micro-targeting and audience manipulation.[6]

Yet, even if we focus simply on the abundance of information, which at times can be overwhelming and confusing, it is clear that we need experts, academics and professionals to engage with social media and to guide users. They must contribute proactively to the rich debate that is taking place on social media platforms across the world and offer their insight and guidance. It is essential that experts help the public to distinguish reputable sources and data from unreliable ones. Experts of all kind must help debunk myths and challenge misinformation. Hence, I encourage all speakers gathered here to be active on social media and to engage with the debates that take place on these platforms.

Our education system, from the early years up to the higher education sector, must engage proactively with this new information environment. We must educate tomorrow's citizens and teach them how to identify reliable sources, data and metadata and to dismiss those that are not. Future generations must know how to navigate the cacophony of opinions and not to be confused or overwhelmed.[7] Our society and our governments must invest more money, time and energy in educating future citizens in the social media age.

Notes

1   Internet Live Stats. Available at: http://www.internetlivestats.com (accessed 14 February 2017).

2   Office of National Statistics, *Internet Access: Households and Individuals: 2016*, 4 August 2016.

3   International Campaign to Abolish Nuclear Weapons. Available at: http://www.icanw.org (accessed 14 February 2017).

4   Office of National Statistics, *Internet Access: Households and Individuals: 2016*, 4 August 2016.

5   'Angela Merkel: Internet search engines are "distorting perception"', *Guardian*, 27 October 2016.

6   See reporting on Cambridge Analytica by Carole Cadwalladr in the *Observer* and the *Guardian*, and by J.J. Payne in *Byline*.

7   Linda Risso, 'Fact checking won't defeat fake news – but education might', *Prospect*, 21 June 2017.

Democracy Is About More Than Voting: Pre-Modern Petitioning and Its Implications for Today

Mark Knights

I want to argue that the nearest pre-modern predecessor of the referendum was the petition – the collection of signatures on parchment or paper that sought to put pressure on Parliament and other institutions. In the past, but particularly in the seventeenth, eighteenth and nineteenth centuries, petitioning raised many of the questions about the relationship between people and their representatives in Parliament that are also raised by the Brexit vote; and petitioning, like the referendum, was often highly contentious. But I argue that petitioning, unlike a referendum, was a ubiquitous and essential part of a vibrant political culture.

Thinking about petitioning is particularly apt not only because of recent massive e-petitions but also because petitioning was key to the original Putney Debates. The Levellers were *a petitioning community* – they used petitions to create political momentum and claimed to speak on behalf of the people. That process challenged authority, even in its revolutionary form of the Army or the Parliament that had been fighting the Crown. Cromwell, as an Army leader, told the Putney Debaters that he feared petitioning would lead to 'utter confusion' because it created multiple and shifting voices in the polity. Petitioning thus posed the challenge, also posed by the Brexit vote, of who best represents the will of the people. Petitioning was a form of informal representation that challenged the formal representative institutions. Inevitably, like Brexit and the referendum, it continually asked deep questions about the nature of popular sovereignty. Like Brexit, it was also deeply contested. Disputes over the right to petition and over what that right entailed if it did exist, persisted over the entire course of the seventeenth, eighteenth and nineteenth centuries.

Why, then, was it so important?

The sociologist David Zaret argues that petitioning in the seventeenth century created the 'origins of democratic culture'. Petitioning was a dialogic process: petition provoked counter-petition, and counter-petition provoked response. It created a political discourse that was very hard to close down.

Mass petitioning was also incredibly extensive and inclusive, even of men and women normally outside the formal political realm, whether or not they had the vote. Huge numbers of people signed petitions. A project being undertaken at Durham University estimates that there were 1 million petitions to Parliament from 1833 to 1918 with 165 million signatures.

Petitioning was also a routine, customary way of doing things – it was not a one-off event, like an election or a referendum, but was embedded in the routine political culture of the pre-modern world. It was constitutionally normal, not abnormal. It could initiate and shape legislation, voice grievances from the parish pump upwards and demand justice.

Moreover, petitioning gave a voice to regions and groups as much as to the nation. Petitions were generated at the local level, representing the views of towns and counties. This gave a regional voice within the national one. And importantly, it enabled the contested *plurality* of the voices of the people to become apparent. One of the problems with the Brexit vote is the idea that the winner takes all, and appeals to *the* voice of the people – as though it only has one – are used to close down debate. Petitioning refused to accept that there was a *single will of the people*. Rather, it revealed many voices of the people, a plurality of legitimate viewpoints that jostled with each other in the public sphere.

Gathering hands to a petition generated political community. The act of assembling to debate, sign and present a petition created community as well as a sense of agency. The abolition of slavery and the repeal of the Corn Laws are good examples of successful pressure, but even when, as was often the case, they did not achieve their ostensible aim, the *process* of petitioning had hugely beneficial consequences for the health of political debate, engagement and activity. It created routinely active citizens and extensive participation that stretched far beyond any periodic vote or poll.

E-petitioning is useful, but it does not achieve all the benefits I have listed. It is petitioning-light, often ephemeral, and does not create the sense of political community that its older form did so well. St Mary's Church, Putney, harbours the echoes of a political culture that, for all its very real limitations and exclusions, was nevertheless refreshing in its vitality, in its ability to represent a diversity of views, and in its sense of ongoing, popular engagement and agency. Such petitioning reminds us that democratic culture is about more than voting.

PART III

Parliament, the Executive, the Courts and the Rule of Law

Does the Separation of Powers Still Work?

Stephen Sedley

Not quite 20 years before the original Putney debates, Sir Edward Coke, now 74 and no longer a judge, took his seat in the House of Commons alongside the great jurist John Selden and a young burgess from East Anglia named Oliver Cromwell. In the course of their debate on the Petition of Right which was to be presented to Charles I, dealing, among other major grievances, with the enforced billeting of troops on civilians, Coke rose to his feet and said:

> Shall the soldier and the justice sit on one bench, the trumpet will not let the crier speak.

Almost four centuries later, we can see what he meant. Not only in the UK but in many other liberal democracies, the demands of security, or perhaps more accurately of the security services, are prioritized over numerous personal freedoms: the soldier's trumpet, in Coke's phrase, drowns the voice of justice.

New and growing, and in many cases arguably necessary, powers of surveillance and restriction granted by elected legislatures have conferred on the security establishment an autonomy which matches, and at some points supersedes, the sovereignty of Parliament, the independence of the judiciary and the authority of the executive – the political trinity which, since the end of the seventeenth century, has come to be recognized as representing the discrete but interlocking building blocks of a democracy.

True, there was never a text or a consensus which decreed this. Locke, for example, while recognizing the need for an impartial judiciary, regarded the bench as a limb of the executive. More important today, however, is the question whether the tripartite allocation of state power is any longer an adequate account of how we are, or should be, governed. At least three elements of the modern state place it in doubt.

One of these, the security establishment, I have already mentioned.

A second is the church – already a major issue in the debates of 1647. From the sixteenth century, with a brief interruption during the years of the republic, the established church has enjoyed a legal status which either places it outside the general law or privileges it within the constitution (not least by placing its 26 senior bishops in the upper house of the legislature). This might be no more than an English eccentricity, like cricket and warm beer, were it not for the fact that, through the incorporation of church schools into the state system, it has led to the institutionalization and protection by law of religious discrimination in public education in ways which would be unconstitutional in, for example, the US or France.

Thirdly, the press. It is now more than two centuries since Burke baptised the press the 'fourth estate' of the realm – meaning that it was next only to the lords, the commons and the clergy in status. Since then, aided by the growth of communication technology, the press has developed a combination of power and autonomy which not only places elements of it on a par with government but enables them to dictate policy to politicians and to attempt to intimidate the judiciary; while every effort at independent external regulation has been brushed aside.

My question therefore is twofold. Firstly, does the traditional tripartite division of the state's powers, with its real or imaginary checks and balances, offer an adequate account of the modern state? And secondly, if it is the case that other major institutions enjoy forms of autonomy which challenge this account, are these developments inexorable, possibly even desirable; or reversible, and if reversible, how?

Are Prerogative Powers Necessary in the Twenty-First Century?

Alison Young

It seems impossible to consider the phrase 'prerogative power' without also mentioning the words 'ancient' and 'monarch'. While these words are needed to explain their origins, this may give the misleading impression that prerogative powers are anachronistic. Yet they perform an important role in the constitution. Prerogative powers are used to enter and withdraw from treaties, to prorogue Parliament, grant honours, to deploy the armed forces and to regulate crown employment contracts – to name but a few. Are they still needed?

It is easy to argue that executive powers are needed. Parliament cannot do everything. Nor should it. We need executive powers to act quickly and expediently.

While Parliament can set broad aims, the executive is needed to impart expert-informed detail, or exercise discretion to ensure fairness. There are also times when the country needs to speak with one voice on the international stage – that voice comes from the government on behalf of Parliament.

That is a case for allowing the executive the power to make and implement rules, but should these be through the royal prerogative? To answer that, we need to understand what makes prerogative powers different from statutory powers. The obvious difference is the source. Prerogatives come from the common law. Statutory powers come from legislation. So, prerogatives can be harder to determine than statutory powers – there may not be a clear text setting out the power delegated to the executive.

There is a difference too, over the regulation of the content of these powers. Legislation can place conditions on the scope or exercise of a statutory power. As shown by the outcome of the *Miller* case, which decided that Parliament rather than the executive had the power to trigger Brexit – the real issue will be over possible amendments to condition the exercise of the power – making it subject to further information, debate, approval before the withdrawal agreement is signed or conditions which prevent the negotiations from removing specific rights. Courts can subject the exercise of statutory powers to judicial review. They determine whether the executive acted within the scope of the powers granted to it by the legislature – the classic action for *ultra vires*. Courts can also control how these powers are exercised – assessing rationality and procedural fairness.

The control over prerogative powers is different. Courts determine their scope. And, as *Miller* makes clear, there are general restrictions on the scope of prerogative powers (you cannot use them to modify common law or statute) as well as issues as to the specific scope of any purported prerogative power. Courts can control the exercise of some – but not all – prerogative powers. They have to be 'justiciable' – suitable for review by the court. Is it too political, or purely discretionary, or does the exercise of the prerogative not really have an impact on domestic law as regulated by the courts?

Why does this matter? Because it touches on the relative role of Parliament and the courts. Do courts have more of a say over the regulation of prerogative powers than statutory powers? If so, is this a problem? It is true that Parliament may have more of a say in the determination of the scope and extent of a statutory power. And courts will pay attention to the wording of

Parliament. However, courts will exercise their powers of review more or less stringently when dealing with both prerogative and statutory powers.

Even if we were concerned to impose greater control over the powers of the executive to Parliament rather than the courts, does Parliament really have the time to identify all of the prerogative powers that we have? What if it missed one? The executive needs to have residual powers to deal with emergency and everyday situations. Does it really make a difference if this is done through a statutory power granting the executive a broad general power to achieve its objectives, or act in an emergency, rather than through relying on prerogative powers?

The real issue here is not whether prerogative powers are needed but whether we should be worried about their existence. As long as we have courts that are willing to act as a check on both statutory and prerogative powers, doing so to protect rights while being sensitive to legitimate, democratically made policy choices, then we do not need to worry about the existence of prerogative powers. And this is the real impact of *Miller* – it demonstrates that the court is willing to protect rights, while remaining sensitive to political choice. However, this also needs Parliament to do its job too, by continuing to hold the government to account.

The Article 50 Legal Challenge: Clarifying the UK's Constitutional Requirements to Start Brexit

Rob Murray

On 24 January 2017, the Supreme Court decided, by a majority of eight judges to three, that the government can only serve notice under Article 50 of the Treaty on European Union (TEU) – the process by which the UK can leave the EU – after an Act of Parliament has been passed. Nothing less will do. This ruling on an ostensibly technical issue made constitutional history in clarifying the extent of the powers of the executive – in this case, the Prime Minister of the UK, Theresa May – and of the UK Parliament.

There was, and remains, a common misconception that this case set out to defy the referendum result and, ultimately, to stop or delay Brexit. Put plainly, it did not; it was about process, not politics. What the aftermath of the referendum had revealed was a staggering lack of clarity concerning the legal procedure to be followed under the UK's constitutional requirements [per Article 50(1) of the TEU] when leaving the EU. Ultimately, to get clarity, this case had to go right to the heart of the application of the fundamental constitutional principles of the separation of powers, parliamentary sovereignty, the independence of the judiciary and the rule of law. This was a necessary process to ensure that the UK leaves lawfully, securing legal certainty before, rather than after, the event.

The central question concerned whether the government can remove a source of domestic constitutional law and/or domestic rights granted by an Act of Parliament and arising under the EU domestic treaty. This was set against a constitutional backdrop in which Parliament is sovereign with respect to the making of laws (other than the common law) but subject to the rule of law as enforced by the courts. The electorate is sovereign politically. Parliamentary sovereignty as regards domestic laws means that the UK must have a dualist constitution: only Parliament can give effect to international treaty rights/obligations in domestic law, as opposed to international rights/obligations as between states under international law, which can be a matter for government.

The key arguments of the lead claimant, Gina Miller, represented by Mishcon de Reya, took the judges back to cases and statutes in the seventeenth century, including the Bill of Rights, which demonstrated that Parliament is sovereign as lawmaker. The residual royal prerogative powers of the government – regarding international relations, and treaties in particular – exist solely in relation to international law rights/obligations. EU rights and obligations are made domestic law by virtue of the European Communities Act 1972 (ECA). Now that the government has triggered Article 50, the notice is irrevocable; once the gun is fired the bullet will hit its target. There will therefore inevitably be a loss of at least some rights in domestic law under the ECA (and which cannot be saved by the Great Repeal Bill). Therefore, only Parliament can grant such a power, and it requires an Act of Parliament to do so.

The parties' cases were like 'ships passing in the night': the government argued that the royal prerogative powers it sought to exercise had always existed, the claimants that they never existed.

The Supreme Court majority agreed with Gina Miller's case and noted that the government's case would lead to perverse results; if correct, it means that the government could always withdraw the UK from the EU without reference to Parliament or a referendum. It could do so even if there was a referendum result in favour of remaining in the EU.

Among the lessons to be learned are that there was, and arguably remains, very considerable ignorance as to the fundamental principles of our constitution, as regards the nature of representative parliamentary sovereignty, the role of referendums and the role of the court in upholding the rule of law. This is a real weakness in our political system which needs to be corrected. On a positive note, the courts managed the whole process in under seven months, a clear indication of the efficiency of our judicial system, which has been noticed both nationally and internationally. And, last but not least, any future referendum will no doubt spell out what, if any, the legal consequences of the result will be.

Enemies of Democracy?
Taking Back Control
through the Courts

Jonathan Lis

On 28th November last year, British Influence proposed a judicial review to challenge the government's belief and intention that we will leave the European Economic Area (EEA) automatically when we exit the EU. The EEA grants membership of the single market to its contracting parties, which include three non-EU member states. Parliament enacted the EEA Act 1993, enshrining the treaty in British domestic law, and the EEA Agreement requires contracting parties to trigger a specific mechanism, Article 127, in order to terminate membership. We suggest that if the government wishes to invoke that and leave the single market, it must first consult

Parliament. It is not an attempt to derail or scupper Brexit.

On 29th November, the *Daily Express* editorial denounced us as 'enemies of democracy'. It opined:

> The tragedy is that if this case is brought it will likely be heard by judges whose own views are firmly pro-EU. It is simply wrong for these important political disputes to be decided in the courts when we have an elected Government acting on direct instructions from a nationwide vote.

I always believed that the full pursuit of democracy required the right to dissent, the right to ensure the government was acting within the law, and the sovereignty of Parliament. Now it seems that the prime minister alone is entitled to determine British people's rights, without any intervention from either Parliament or an apparently biased and untrustworthy judiciary. Democracy now means doing as you are told: an endeavour to empower not citizens, but the government.

But citizens are key. Both the EEA challenge and the *Miller* case humanize Brexit's political dramas by focusing on individuals' rights: principally, the reciprocal rights to work, settle and trade freely in other member states. Both cases contend that only Parliament can remove those rights, not the government by royal prerogative. Indeed, following *Miller*, Parliament has voted to do so by enabling the invocation of Article 50. The High Court and Supreme Court did not seek to safeguard those rights: quite the reverse, they conferred upon Parliament the full authority to terminate them. In a sense, then, the Brexit mantra of 'taking back control' was duly fulfilled by a sovereign Parliament empowered by judicial intervention. But what of those British – and indeed EU and EEA citizens – who consider that they are to lose rights and lose control?

Lady Thatcher once informed a colleague of mine that 'we don't need human rights because we have the House of Commons'. But what happens when the Commons does not grant or guarantee rights, but in fact withdraws them? European infrastructure determines that human rights transcend national sovereignty; according to Parliament, the UK is bound by both the EU's Charter of Fundamental Rights, and the European Convention on Human Rights, enforced by courts in Luxembourg and Strasbourg, respectively. It is now government policy to leave the former as part of Brexit, and the latter – a brainchild of Churchill – sometime subsequently. Just as British courts have not sought to preserve EU rights, they may in the future have no obligation – or indeed no mandate – to enforce human rights either. Sovereignty and control rest with Parliament, and we must hope Parliament remains benign.

So what of the enemies of democracy? In the last lines of *King Lear*, Britain's new leader Edgar signals renewal after tragedy and despotism thus: 'The weight of this sad time we must obey, / Speak what we feel, not what we ought to say.' The media and government discourse on Brexit has emphatically rejected his advice. For politicians and commentators in particular, dissent has been recast as treason. To question a vote won narrowly after a campaign of deliberate misinformation – even to question the details of its implementation – is to subvert the will of the people. High-profile figures who challenge the details of Brexit are threatened with physical violence – particularly if they are female, non-white or not British-born. To say what they feel about Brexit is to say the unsayable.

Previously, 'saying the unsayable' was the demand – made in the name of free speech – of political fringes to defy norms protecting marginalized groups. Today, those now-mainstream fringes jealously guard the new politically correct orthodoxies and denounce challenges to them as anti-democratic. Enemies of democracy are the famed 'liberal elite', 'Remoaners' of ill repute who, criminally, have continued to speak despite losing, and have opposed the rapid introduction of a radical state-sanctioned groupthink.

If judges are enemies of the people, and those who seek legal redress are enemies of democracy, then democracy loses its meaning. It becomes an unwelcome parasite on the body politic, separate from and unloved by the people it needs to serve. If democracy is co-opted to delegitimize the views of 48 per cent of voters, we enable the tyranny not only of the majority, but of democracy itself.

The Role of Experts in Parliamentary Democracy

David Vines

Who needs experts when we all have our own opinions?

This is the ethos of Facebook. According to this ethos, it is important to have an opinion, much more important than to have knowledge. Even better is to go viral with one's opinion.

This is a chilling ethos. The opinions formed on social media are so ill-informed, so fragile and so volatile. Here is an example. There was news recently on the BBC that the UK and New Zealand plan a Free Trade deal as soon as possible after Brexit. A friend of mine – who does much tweeting – thought that this fact was ridiculously unimportant, since trade between the UK and New Zealand is so small. He thought that he would send a tweet to point this out. So he tweeted as follows. 'This will not make much difference. That is because we export 200 times more to the EU than to New Zealand'. This tweet produced 2,000 retweets. So then he tried again. 'We do much more trade with the EU in two days then we do with New Zealand in a whole year'. This was retweeted 315,000 times. It is clear from this example – and from everything that we know – that the effects of experts on the opinions of citizens are very fragile if they are acquired through social media.

How are we, the experts, to respond to this difficulty? Here is a response put forward recently by Matthew Flinders, Professor of Politics at the University of Sheffield, who leads a Centre studying the Public Understanding of Politics. Professor Flinders responded, in a recent article in *Prospect* magazine, by saying that academics need to respond by undergoing more training in the art of translation: more training in what he calls 'engaged scholarship'.

In my view this is a craven response. I say this because such a response fails to respect the fundamental ideas that underpin parliamentary democracy, ideas which are so important to all of us here. But what are these ideas? And if I am so dismissive, then what else is needed?

Our parliamentary democracy is a representative democracy, not a delegate democracy. That is why what Flinders says is so inadequate. In a representative democracy, experts have an essential role to play not as engaged persons, but as persons with knowledge. Their role is to provide the best possible advice to those who, in our representative democracy, make decisions on our behalf. Experts do have such an ability to give such best possible advice. The world is a complicated place about which, on any given topic, most of us know much too little. Experts spend their lives finding out what makes sense in the field in which they specialize. The professional career of being an expert is to be someone who acquires such knowledge. We should be able to trust experts to acquire this knowledge in a professional manner, and to use this knowledge to provide the best possible advice. Such advice will make use of both their ability and their knowledge.

Experts are located in a number of places, including, especially, in universities. Some of the other places in which they can be found are, at first glance, surprising. I was speaking recently to the Rector of the College of Europe in Bruges about the Putney Debates 2017 held at St Mary's Church. He made a particularly thoughtful remark about the role that the House of Lords plays in

Britain's parliamentary system. Members of the House of Lords are not governed by the normal rules of political engagement, including the need to perpetually work toward being re-elected. They have time to listen to experts and to think about what they hear. As a result, many of them, the Rector said, become experts themselves.

You might well think that I am just special pleading. That I am simply an academic who wants to be taken seriously as an expert. And is not my particular position a peculiar one, given that the reputation of economists has taken such a beating since the global financial crisis. Many, many people have criticized economists for failing to predict that crisis. Why should we think of them as experts?

I do think my position is defensible. In my view, economists are not able to *predict* outcomes, they can only forecast them. The mistake of economists – and it was a real one – was to dress up their ideas in precise mathematical models and then to claim that they could use these models to predict outcomes. No medic can predict whether you will die of cancer, and if so when. A cancer specialist can only *forecast*. The most he can do is to tell his patient the probability of falling foul of that disease, to the best of his ability, and to explain what things the patient could do to lower that probability. Nobody, standing by in 1810, could have predicted the outcome of the Battle of Waterloo. But a good historian might have had a worthwhile view about where that battle was likely to take place and what the outcome was likely to be. No economist could have predicted the global financial crisis. But economists should have warned about the likely outcome, and should have advised about the measures necessary to avoid such an outcome. Good economists did warn and advise in such a manner.

So let me act as an expert. Let me warn and let me give advice in my own area of expertise. I believe that the Brexit vote by the British public was a vote to be made much worse off. Expert economists warned of this fact at the time. And I am advising that Brexit will cause this to happen now, unless, somehow, a hard Brexit is avoided. I say this partly because I am an Australian. Australians have much experience that is relevant for Britain at present.

In the last 30 years Australia has suffered on a number of occasions from significant reductions in the global demand for its exports, not least currently, when the prices of iron ore and coal have fallen because of a reduction of economic growth in China. I believe that something like this will happen to the UK, as and when a hard Brexit reduces our ability to sell financial services, motor cars and many other products to consumers in Europe. In Australia something like this happened most notably at the time of the Asian financial crisis in 1997–8. Australia's major export markets in Asia collapsed. But within months, Australia's currency was allowed to depreciate by 30 per cent. Australia's exports to the rest of the world grew spectacularly fast: exports to the US went up by 30 per cent in one year. This meant that Australia went on growing. Other countries, in particular Canada and New Zealand, acted to prevent the fall of their currency and thereby created a large increase in unemployment. The Australian Central Bank, the Reserve Bank, knew what to do. The economy was well managed and unemployment – and a recession – was avoided, because the Reserve Bank engineered a depreciation of the currency. But the real income of Australians suffered; imports cost much, much more. And ordinary Australians wanting to travel abroad for holidays basically had to give up and stay at home.

My advice is this. I believe that a hard Brexit will mean that something like this is likely to happen in Britain. I believe that the British economy is well managed by the Bank of England, in the same way that the

Australian economy is well managed by the Australian Reserve Bank. The Bank of England will not allow the collapse in European demand for our exports to lead to unemployment. And the way that it will bring this about is by causing the pound to fall by much more than it has fallen already. That is how and why those in Britain will be made much worse off by a hard Brexit.

I say all this, using my expert knowledge of international economics. Notice that I am not going viral to tweet what I believe will be the outcome. And notice that, in telling you this now, I am also not engaging in what Professor Flinders would describe as 'engaged scholarship'. I am telling you this now because I consider myself to be an expert in relation to this sort of subject matter in international economics. I believe that it is my professional obligation to tell you what I believe to be the likely outcome, in this area in which I have enough knowledge to be considered an expert. In a well-functioning representative democracy such expert advice would be listened to. Of course, such expert advice might be contested by other experts. But it would be taken more seriously than has happened up until now in Britain.

The UK's Institutional Balance of Power After Leaving the EU

Michael Dougan

When lawyers talk about 'Europeanization', they are referring to the impact upon the national legal system of EU membership – both direct (e.g., the introduction of new regulatory frameworks in fields such as trade or the environment) and indirect (e.g., the spillover effects of EU influence into what are formally purely national fields of responsibility).

But perhaps the most important impact is on the institutional balance of power between the branches of domestic government.

According to the traditional story, the main winners of Europeanization are the courts, in their relations with both Parliament and the executive. The courts are endowed with a wider range of powers to find state action unlawful. They are entrusted with more penetrating powers of scrutiny over state policy choices, especially through the principle of proportionality. They have strong obligations to ensure the effective judicial protection of individual citizens in their relations with state authority. And of course, they are empowered to disapply primary legislation, in certain circumstances, where it is incompatible with the state's obligations under the EU treaties.

But equally: in a constitutional system such as the UK, where the government already almost entirely dominates Parliament, EU membership has also exacerbated the continuing growth of national executive power at the expense of national legislative power – a situation only partially compensated for by the increasing role of the European Parliament or indeed (particularly since the Treaty of Lisbon) of the national parliaments being more directly involved in EU-level affairs.

Those two phenomena are not unrelated: for many, the bolstering of executive power helps to explain and indeed justify the magnification of judicial scrutiny, so as to help ensure that governmental authority is better held to account, and so as to protect the interests of economic and social minorities.

Against that background, the question now arises: what will 'de-Europeanization' look like? What happens when you take away the necessary sources of those direct and indirect influences upon your national constitutional and legal arrangements? What will be the more long-lasting legacies of 40-plus years of EU membership? And what new dynamics of change, both direct and indirect, will withdrawal create for itself?

As with almost everything else, there are no answers to those questions. The referendum, government and now Parliament have unleashed a process whose direction is unknown, and whose possibilities are highly contested, but whose transformative potential is enormous.

But already, we can see some crucially important moments when government and Parliament will have at least to start showing their hands. For example, within months, the UK will begin the process of deciding which EU rights and obligations are to be retained, reformed or abolished – under the so-called Great Repeal Bill and beyond.

How will Parliament respond to this new environment? How far will it find the necessary skills, resources, independence and confidence to strengthen its mechanisms for government accountability and exercise greater power over legislative policymaking?

Or how far will the culture of executive dominance continue, as much outside the EU as within it?

And how will our courts adjust to life, without the direct tools of scrutiny and intervention which had been provided to them for so long by the EU? Will they be willing simply to relinquish their power to police the proportionality of government action, or their duty to furnish the citizen with effective judicial protection? Or will they find ingenuous ways to resurrect some of those old powers, through the unwritten codes of common law jurisprudence? Perhaps even carrying further down the line of challenging for themselves the full force of the traditional doctrine of parliamentary sovereignty?

For me – this is where the real significance of the *Miller* ruling lies. Its impact on the basic decision to withdraw was only ever going to be marginal. Its lasting importance perhaps lies in setting the 'constitutional tone' for what comes next – the mood music, as it were, for how the institutions of state should understand their own and each others' roles in the far-reaching processes to follow. So on the one hand, we see a strong affirmation of parliamentary power relative to governmental authority. But on the other hand, the Supreme Court stressed that it was for Parliament to decide what to actually do with that power – perhaps placing overly high hopes on the capacity and willingness of Parliament to assume anything more than a formal (rather than a more substantive and meaningful) role.

As if trying to answer such questions was not already complicated enough, we should not forget a whole range of additional variables that will come into play: for example, how far the shameless dishonesty of the Leave campaign will tarnish the quality of our national public life for years to come; whether the political tensions produced by the referendum and now withdrawal will fragment existing political party structures and voter allegiances; what will happen to devolution – including the structures of English regional governance?

And of course, we should not pretend that all of the answers will be matters of choice: some variables will be decided for us, not by us. What will be the domestic consequences of being excluded from so many of the structures through which European countries seek to solve collective problems – through shared policymaking and the dissemination of good practice? How will the relationship between public and private power change, once the UK is obliged to engage with global concentrations of economic might, all on our little own, rather than through the medium of the

EU – and how will that affect the role and balance of our own state institutions?

We cannot directly provide the real life answers to these fundamental questions. Our job is to identify the relevant issues – to understand them more thoroughly, to criticize them more rigorously and even perhaps to help shape some better outcomes. By the way: that does not make us 'enemies of the people' – a thoroughly despicable assault on scientific expertise and freedom of expression by political dogmatists whose definition of democracy is entirely selective and self-serving. In any case, one thing is crystal clear: leaving the EU is about transforming the UK as much internally as externally – as much about rewriting the rules of our own politics, economy and society, as it is about just leaving the EU.

PART IV

Preserving the Liberal Constitution

Voice and Vote

Timothy Garton Ash

In a famous passage from the original Putney Debates, Colonel Thomas Rainsborough declares that 'the poorest he that is in England hath a life to live, as the greatest he', that government requires individual consent, and that 'I do think that the poorest man in England is not at all bound in a strict sense to that government that he hath not had a voice to put himself under'. Rainsborough says *voice* where we might expect the word vote. Assuming that his contemporary William Clarke's shorthand notes of the debate on 29 October 1647 are accurate – and this is not a piece of 'fake news' from the seventeenth century – we have here a classic English statement of the inextricable connection between democracy and free speech. It is no accident that in several languages the same word is used for voice and vote: *Stimme* in German, *glos* in Polish, *sawt* in Arabic. Free speech is an indispensable part of the constitution of liberty.

At least three things follow for post-Brexit England. Firstly, watch out for anyone who claims to speak in the name of the People, especially with a capital P. How many times in recent weeks have we heard that 'the people have spoken', that Parliament and the courts must bow before 'the will of the people', otherwise they will be 'enemies of the people' – for the *Daily Mail*, you see, has an exclusive hotline to the almighty People. This is the classic deceit of contemporary populism: the attributed voice of the singular People trumps (the verb has already acquired a new meaning) all other sources of legitimate authority. But are not the 48 per cent of us who voted for Britain to stay in the EU also people? If not people, then what? We are a part, a very substantial part, of the people. What distinguishes a liberal from an illiberal democracy is that the people are plural, there are other peoples of England, Scotland, Wales and Northern Ireland and we the citizens speak in many individual voices, not a single one ventriloquized by Nigel Farage, Boris Johnson or the *Daily Mail*.

Secondly, democracy requires not just free speech in the abstract but a particular ecosystem of communication. Ideally, this will permit the deliberative democracy that happened in St Mary's Church 370 years ago – everyone listening to each other's arguments, even Cromwell and the bolshie Rainsborough, and disagreeing with robust civility – to be reproduced in necessarily virtual spaces on the scale of a whole country. This requires media that give you the whole range of competing arguments, honestly presented, with evidence, including facts that are actually facts, not factoids or what Trump's adviser Kellyanne Conway memorably called 'alternative facts'. No media can live up entirely to this ideal, and the *BBC Today* programme generally still does a great job (and I hope will continue to do so under its new editor). But what we saw in the Brexit campaign, with its constantly repeated lies, its fake news ('Queen backs Brexit'), online echo chambers, contempt for experts and simplistic narrative prevailing over complex reality, is that we are beginning to lose the media we need for democratic self-government. A liberal constitution will not survive unless it is embedded in an ecosystem of uncensored, diverse and trustworthy media – and that is endangered in England now.

Thirdly, if we are to have a written constitution, as I believe we should, then it must include something like the US First Amendment – which was, incidentally, born from the heritage of seventeenth-century English Puritans. Thomas Rainsborough's brother-in-law was John Winthrop, the one who declared that what they called New England should be 'as a City upon a Hill'. Well, let *old* England now be as a City upon a Hill, and *our* free speech guarantee should be not a subsequent Amendment but a foundational article of a modern liberal constitution, high up among the most important articles, as in several European constitutions, but composed in our own English words, echoing the great language of our seventeenth-century predecessors: plain, clear, robust and muscular.

Plurinational Democracy

Michael Keating

The Putney Debates mark a key point in the early emergence of English democracy and civil equality. They are also part of the birth of the English nation as a political society. Revisionist historians may have reinterpreted them as part of a European phenomenon and noted that the Scots and Irish had more than walk-on parts in the events of that era, but the English frame has left a lasting legacy. On one side Brexit campaigners evoke a history of sovereign democracy and call for taking back control. On the other, progressives talk of a people's constitutional convention to design a new constitution for the nation, based on shared values and meanings, to be endorsed by a UK-wide referendum.

Such calls rest upon a profound misunderstanding of the state in which we live. The UK is not a unitary state and people but a union of nations, understood differently in its various parts. While English understandings of democracy and nationhood are profoundly unitary, in Scotland they are multilayered and plural. The constitutional settlement in Northern Ireland rests upon the legitimation and concrete expression of multiple identities and understandings of sovereignty. Even constitutional law differs from one part of the union to another. Any constitutional settlement for the UK must recognize this complexity, the absence of a unitary people (*demos*) and the impossibility of a shared *telos* in the form of a common view of the state and its future. This does not mean that constitutionalism is impossible but that it must take a particular form.

In this, the UK more resembles the EU than it does a nation state. The EU, too, lacks a unitary demos and telos and is understood in multiple ways. While it has never been a good fit with the unitary, English conception of the polity, it is a remarkably good counterpart to the UK understood as union.

Brexit highlights these differing understandings of the polity. While the Brexiteers proposed taking sovereignty back to one place (although it is not clear whether this is to be the Parliament or the people), research in Scotland has shown that most people are quite happy for it to be shared at multiple levels – even independence supporters. The Northern Ireland settlement has worked by deliberately incorporating multiple sovereignties, and polls in recent years suggest that this, rather than Irish unity, is the preferred option, even for Catholics. It is hardly surprising that both Scotland and Northern Ireland voted to remain in the EU.

Events since the referendum suggest that, in the capital, the UK is still seen as a unitary state and people. There is an insistence, dressed in the language of democracy and popular sovereignty, that a vote of the whole state must prevail over the preferences of its components; the Conservatives and Labour appear united on this. The Supreme Court, called on to decide whether the government needed parliamentary approval to commence the process of withdrawal, was also asked about the implications for the nations of the UK. The Scottish government argued that, under the Sewel Convention, legislation in devolved spheres or changes in the powers of the devolved legislatures would require the consent of those bodies; Brexit would therefore require it too. The Court, not content with arguing that Brexit was a reserved matter or that the Convention only applied in 'normal' circumstances, chose to declare that the Convention was a mere 'political' matter with no binding force whatever. At a stroke, this denied 20 years of constitutional development.

Efforts to reclaim and deepen democracy can draw on the legacy of Putney, but they must go beyond that, to recognize our plurinational context and how the popular will is expressed beyond the unitary nation state. None of this suggests that basic values differ among the peoples of these islands, but nor are the common values necessarily British or resting upon unified identity. Calls for the assertion of British values almost invariably refer to values that are universal. The point is that the contexts for the realization of these values and the political community in which they are given expression are varied and plural as are the *demoi* (peoples) in democracy.

These considerations also affect the case for a written constitution for the UK. There might appear to be strong democratic justifications for such a constitution. Yet it would be a serious mistake to try and provide a definitive answer to the UK's constitutional predicament when this is so deeply contested both by the contrasting starting points and aspirations of the peoples of these islands and by the very different attitudes to the European project. Constitutionalism is better practised as a conversation around different conceptions rather than the imposition of a single design, whether that be unitary or federal.

Judeo-Christian Principles Underlying the Constitution

Ailsa Newby

In 1647, the first recorded discussion in England of the constitution of a democratic government took place in St Mary's Church, Putney.

The matrix for the 1647 debate included the assumptions that only men had a voice or a role to play in government and that the underlying principles must inevitably be drawn from Christianity.

Last year, in commemoration of Magna Carta, we asked that question again in this church: What does good government look like now? And, because we live in a multi-faith society where men and women are (at least notionally) regarded as equal, we redressed the balance of debate in this place a little by asking three eminent women theologians to account for their views. A Muslim, a Jew and a Christian. They were Sughra Ahmed, President of the Muslim Council of Great Britain, Rabbi Julia Neuberger and June Osborne, Dean of Salisbury.

What emerged from what they said was the common ground. That the core role of good government is to promote human flourishing. For that flourishing human beings need to be protected from the abuse of power. Humans matter.

For Christians, that principle is embodied in the opening chapter of the Hebrew Bible and so seminal too in the Jewish tradition.

> God created humankind in his image,
> in the image of God he created them;
> male and female he created them.[1]

Humans are created male and female in the image of God. From this comes logically a principle of the inherent value of every individual; and the equality of every individual. Needless to say, this has not always been honoured in the structures of human society – I think of the priest John Ball in the Peasants' Revolt:

> When Adam delved and Eve span who was then the gentleman?

And of course reflected in the statement of Colonel Rainsborough in this church:

the poorest he that is in England hath a life to live as the greatest he

Yet the valuing of each and every human being does not of itself give you a route map to its achievement. As John Rees reminded us earlier, the Rainsborough quote goes on to say:

> I think it's clear, that every man that is to live under a government ought first by his own consent to put himself under that government; and I do think that the poorest man in England is not bound in a strict sense to that government that he hath not had a voice to put himself under.

So the principle is clear: all should have a say in who governs them. The difficulty, of course, is the praxis. Colonel Rainsborough himself excluded half of the human race from his vision as he talked of 'men' – definitely not used as a synonym for humanity!

There is a classic prayer originating from the Book of Common Prayer which prays: 'Guide this and every nation in the ways of justice and of peace that all may honour one another and seek the common good.'

The reality is, though, that human beings do not always work for the common good, or may misunderstand what is meant by the common good.

In Christian terms, this has been summed up by the former Bishop of Oxford, now a cross-bench peer, Richard Harries – that we are 'made in the image of God and a violator of that image'.[2] That humanity get things wrong must be recognized.

That is reflected too in the famous maxim of Reinhold Neibhur, a protestant theologian: 'Man's capacity for justice makes democracy possible; but man's inclination to injustice makes democracy necessary.'[3] As a US citizen of German heritage in the 1930s and 1940s, he had reason to know. It is wise to remember that Hitler's rise to power was enabled by the popular vote in a referendum.

So I want to say that checks and balances are needed – because power can corrupt. Others are much better qualified than me to say what the checks and balances are – but they obviously include the rule of law, the entrenchment of human rights and the separation of powers. Power can corrupt. Short-term expediency can be the order of the day.

So humans should strive for equality and the common good; and yet, because they tend to fail, constraints are necessary. Will Parliament stand up courageously to the executive and MPs be more than puppets for the party machine?

To end, I want to draw us back to discussion of the profound divisions in society that have been thrown up in the last year: between richer and poorer; between educated and less-educated; between North and South.

The poorest he has a life to live as the greatest he –

Easy to state, hard to achieve. Do we have the systems to achieve it? Can we expect our constitution to work well, if there is profound social and economic inequality? How do you create the checks and balances so that all may honour one another and seek the common good?

Notes

1   Genesis 1:27.
2   Bryan T. McGraw, *Faith in Politics: Religion and Liberal Democracy* (Cambridge: Cambridge University Press, 2010), p. 69.
3   Reinhold Neibuhr, *The Children of Light and the Children of Darkness* (London: Nisbet, 1945), p. vi.

Why the UK Needs a Written Constitution

A.C. Grayling

A state has a constitution, whether it is written or unwritten. It specifies the nature of the state's institutions, their duties, the extent and limit of their powers, the inter-relationships between them and the responsibilities of their officers. And it specifies the relationship between the state and its citizens.

In a written constitution these matters are codified, and means are provided for judicial review of whether the constitution's provisions are being properly applied. In an unwritten constitution these matters are regulated by custom and tradition, together with such statute as has been adopted to supplement or regularize the customs where changing conditions have made this necessary.

The virtues of a written constitution are clarity and definiteness. The virtue of an unwritten constitution is flexibility. The vices of each are the opposites of the respective virtues. Critics of written constitutions point to the stipulative difficulty of amending the constitution. Critics of unwritten constitutions point to their vulnerability to changing interpretations from which there is no appeal, the changes prompted perhaps by expediency or partisanship.

An implication of these remarks is that a written constitution constrains government in ways that an unwritten constitution does not. The government is subject to it, whereas with an unwritten constitution it is the constitution which is subject to the government; the government can choose to alter it or interpret it in ways that suits itself. A written constitution is therefore an important safeguard against abuses by government of their powers, not least because it would entrench civil liberties and the due processes of law.

This last is one of the chief considerations in favour of a written constitution. In the UK, the Human Rights Act (HRA) goes some way to entrenching citizens' liberties, but because it does not give the Supreme Court power to strike down legislation, or restrain government action which is at odds with the

HRA, the effect is not as powerful as a fully written constitution.

Those who say that a written constitution would be too rigid because amending it would be more onerous than amending or repealing statute law are in fact indicating a virtue: a constitution not at the whim of any current administration is a sterner guardian of rights and liberties than a constitution malleable to partisan and passing interests. Moreover, devising careful and consensual means for amending a constitution when changing circumstances make a powerful case for doing so cannot be beyond human ingenuity. The inflexibility of the US Constitution is the result of treating it as if it were holy writ rather than a document serving a nation's needs.

Those who say that an unwritten constitution allows democratic demand to shape the constitutional arrangements of the state, rather than vesting the power to interpret them in a Supreme Court, likewise miss an important point – that if constitutional change requires a supermajority in Parliament, or in a referendum, the change will be truly democratic, and will avoid the dangers pointed out by J.S. Mill as implicit in crude majoritarianism.

The argument that parliamentary sovereignty would be abolished by having a written constitution is intended to suggest that this would be a bad thing. In fact, Parliament is not sovereign de facto; the executive is. As the executive is drawn form the majority in Parliament, the whipping system of party discipline means that the executive is guaranteed to get its way, its party's members serving as lobby fodder to that end, in violation of the explicit duty of MPs to put the interests of their constituents and the country before all else – including before their party's interests.

In any event, with an unwritten constitution and the putative sovereignty of Parliament, a single-vote majority in the House of Commons can result in any violation of constitutional tradition or citizens' liberties – a degree of arbitrary power that is not acceptable in a diverse and complex modern society where most interests are minority interests and require protection.

Thoughts from Across the Pond: The US Constitution (1787, 2017)

Richard W. Clary

The US Constitutional Debate

The United States' own Putney Debates moment was the constitutional convention of 1787, at which we too deliberated the proper roles of the executive and the legislature and debated the merits and weaknesses of direct democracy versus deliberative democracy and the proper role of the representative in a representative government. It is important to view those debates in historical context and then to assess the results: a written constitution that carefully laid out a structure of checks and balances, both explicit and implicit, vertical and horizontal.

The historical context for the American constitutional debate was somewhat different from the English experience. The war for independence from Great Britain ended with the signing of the Treaty of Paris in 1783, negotiated on the American side principally by John Jay, one of our seven Founding Fathers. The treaty was ratified the following year by the Continental Congress. The treaty expressly recognized each of the 13 colonies – now the 13 states – to be free, sovereign, independent states.

Our operating governing document at that time was the 'Articles of Confederation and Perpetual Union', which was essentially a treaty among the 13 states. The United States of America was described as a 'league of friendship'. The Articles established a Congress (a legislature) based on the premise of state equality – one state, one vote. That Congress had minimal powers, with no power over commerce, and no ability to tax. There was no executive, and no national judiciary. With the ratification of the Treaty of Paris and the complete removal of the British monarchy from the scene, something had to fill the void.

What emerged from the 1787 debates was a written constitution describing a new national government, with legislative, executive and judicial branches, that had explicit delineated powers over commerce, taxation, war and peace, treaties, the military and so forth, distributed in a manner designed to force deliberation and compromise, and with built-in checks and balances to guard against overreach by any branch. The debates were held over four months behind closed doors and shuttered windows, largely away from the scrutiny of the public and the press, in order to encourage free debate and compromise. Notes were kept, but the votes of individual delegates were not identified so as to make it easier for each delegate to change his mind as the deliberations continued. That secrecy no doubt played a role in the success of the debates.

Political Theories and Practical Realities

The drafters of the constitution had to contend with several undercurrents of concerns. Chief among these was a concern by the smaller states that the larger states would use a stronger national government to run roughshod over their interests. Another concern was substantial distrust of potential tyranny by an executive – the substitution of an American king for a British one. Also, there was substantial distrust of the potential tyranny of the majority over the rights of the minority, although in this case the 'rights of the minority' referred principally to the property rights of wealthy white males.

The Federalists – the winning side in the debates – distrusted direct democracy. In Federalist Papers No. 10, written as part of the campaign to ratify the constitution, James Madison discussed how in direct democracy, the majority may – indeed, will – 'sacrifice to its ruling passion or interest both the public good and the rights of other citizens.' Madison, John Jay and others saw the solution in a republican form of government – 'the delegation of ... government ... to a small number of citizens elected by the rest.' The benefit of representative government would be

> to refine and enlarge the public views, by passing them through the medium of a chosen body of citizens, whose wisdom may best discern the true interest of their country, and whose patriotism and love of justice will be least likely to sacrifice it to temporary or partial considerations. Under such a regulation, it may well happen that the public voice, pronounced by the representatives of the people, will be more consonant to the public good than if pronounced by the people themselves, convened for the purpose.

Thus Madison, Jay and others made the case for *deliberative democracy*, with the deliberations passed through the *filter* of wise, independent representatives tasked with ascertaining the common good based on better information and informed debate, even if the result is inconsistent with the less informed, less deliberative, passion-based opinions of the public at large. The representative was a better source for deciding what the constituents *should* want if they had the benefits of the same time, knowledge and deliberations as the representative.

The Resulting Structure

These political theories had to be combined with the practical realities of 13 individual sovereign states, with compromises producing the American Constitution.

The consent of the governed was recognized by the preamble – 'We the People' – and achieved by the requirement of ratification by each state through specifically called constitutional conventions.

The *legislative* powers were split between two chambers: (1) The *House of Representatives* had its membership divided among the 13 states based on population and its members elected directly by the relevant voters of each state. This chamber had the most direct connection with and most frequent accountability to the citizens. (2) The House shared legislative powers with the *Senate*, its membership distributed equally by state – two senators for each state – and its members selected by the legislature of each state. (Direct election of senators would not happen until 1913, with the passage of the 17th Amendment.) Senators were intended to be selected for their knowledge and deliberative powers, men of education and presumably wealth. Their method of selection and longer term of office removed the senators from the perceived uninformed passions of the citizens.

The people were to be even further removed from selecting the *executive*. The method of the president's selection was carefully designed both to remove it from uninformed passion and to maintain in some respect the balance of powers among the states. Thus, each state was awarded a number of electors equal to its number of representatives and senators combined. Two filters applied to the selection process: each state's legislature would pick the electors, chosen specifically for the purpose based on their wisdom and reputation, and then the electors would gather together in their respective 13 states, all on the same day, to independently deliberate, nominate and vote for president. All 13 sets of results were to be sent to the president of the Senate, who would add them up and announce the winner. The intention was that the electors, specially selected for their independent judgement, would nominate and elect the best candidate to be president, quite far removed from public opinion and free of foreign influence.

Finally, the constitution established a national *judiciary*, to be a check on both the president and the legislature. The *Bill of Rights* was quickly added in 1791, ten amendments to make clear the limitations on the powers of the new national government and to identify critical rights for the citizens.

The result was an idealistic form of government we have rather loosely referred to since as a 'democracy' and as a 'republic', reflected in the names of our two major political parties today. What the Founding Fathers failed to appreciate was how partisan politics and the aggressive rise of factions – the political parties – would stress and ultimately change this ideal.

The Constitutional Future of the UK: 'Matters of High Concernment'

D.J. Galligan

I

In the seventeenth century, constitutional matters were commonly expressed in terms of the body politic by analogy to the body human. The body politic like the body human can be in good health or poor. The very word 'constitution' has a double meaning, for as well as referring to the rules of government, it indicates good or poor health. To be in good constitution is to be in good health. The body politic is in good health if it functions well, providing good and effective government in which the people acquiesce. In the seventeenth century, many, including parliamentarians and the Levellers, held the body politic to be in poor health or poor constitution, and needed to be restored to good health or constitution.

By the mid-eighteenth century, after major changes and upheavals, David Hume declared the balanced constitution to be near perfect, and the body politic restored to excellent health. Whether recent constitutional events signal a decline in the well-being of the nation is a matter of opinion, and opinions differ. That the relationship between the people and Parliament, between rulers and ruled, has been rendered uncertain is plain. And since that relationship is the very heart of the body politic, there is cause for concern and a case for review. The purpose of the Putney Debates 2017, recorded in these pages, was to examine the patient, make a diagnosis and prescribe remedies. That on such matters opinions remain divided is not surprising; in constitutional affairs that is in the nature of things. If opinions, whatever course they take, are even slightly better informed as a result of the Debates, and this accompanying volume, our purpose will have been achieved.

II

The concept of parliamentary sovereignty, which means the Queen-in-Parliament is the supreme lawmaker, was born and bred in the House of Commons in the late eighteenth century, and continues to be a foundation of the Constitution of the United Kingdom. Among the three institutions of State, the powers of the monarch and peers have shrunk as those of the House of Commons have grown, to make it the effective wielder of constitutional authority. It is elected by the people, but it is not the agent or delegate of the people; nor may it act under the direction or instructions of electors. The House of Commons is instead a representative body, the principal duty of which is to act for the good of the nation, formerly called the common weal, now sometimes expressed as the common good, at other times the public interest. The people have no standing constitutionally to control the actions of the House of Commons, except the right from time to time to vote on its membership.

The representative form of government, along the lines drawn in the UK and elsewhere, is now common to a majority of the world's national and State constitutions. In designing the Constitution of the United States of America in the late eighteenth century, James Madison adopted a form of republicanism based on the representative principle, which he explained as 'the delegation of the government … to a small number of citizens elected by the rest'. The justification follows:

> the effect [is] to refine and enlarge the public views, by passing them through the medium of a chosen body of citizens, whose wisdom may best discern the true interest of their country, and whose patriotism and love of justice will be least likely to sacrifice it to temporary or partial considerations.

Consequences follow:

> Under such a regulation, it may well happen that the public voice, pronounced by the representatives of the people, will be more consonant to the public good than if pronounced by the people themselves, convened for the purpose.

But there are risks:

> On the other hand, the effect may be inverted. Men of factious tempers, of local prejudices, or of sinister designs, may, by intrigue, by corruption, or by other means, first obtain the suffrages, and then betray the interests, of the people.

Although such risks are unavoidable, Madison went on to propose ways of guarding against them and warned of the need for vigilance on the part of the people to make sure their representatives use well the authority entrusted to them.

At the time Madison wrote, British parliamentarians and commentators were engaged with similar matters: how to define the relationship between the people and Parliament. From among the different views expressed inside the Commons and outside, Parliament settled on a form of representative government, expressed as the sovereignty of Parliament. Despite differences in language, the notion of representative government implicit in parliamentary sovereignty is similar to that adopted by Madison and his supporters; it has now become the standard form of constitutional authority. It offers a practical resolution of the tension between two competing ideas: that the people should be in some sense in charge of their own affairs; and the need for good and effective government.

Nevertheless, the relationship between the people and Parliament, rulers and ruled, is inherently unstable. It depends on opinion, on the opinion not just of the rulers and their supporters, but, as Hume noted, on the opinion of the people. And as opinion shifts and changes, the relationship between the two may need to be adjusted. As a practical principle of political life, the people are inclined to accept or acquiesce in the existing constitutional order, whatever its frustrations and imperfections. But loyalty has its limits and must compete with other expectations and inclinations, and may be stretched beyond endurance. From the course of constitutional history, punctuated by episodes of restlessness, rebellion and sometimes revolution, we are able to detect the signs of popular disaffection. And as history teaches, when such signs are plainly visible, the body politic may not be in good health and remedies may need to be prescribed, if worse is to be avoided.

III

Turning now to current events, we should consider whether such signs are appearing here in the UK and elsewhere. The referendum, and the attitude of members of the House of Commons towards it; the manifest disaffection on the part of the people or sections of the people; the questioning of fundamental features of the liberal, rights-based constitution; the apparent demand for stronger executive authority; the claim of sovereignty of the people – all strengthen the case for reflection on the present constitutional settlement and whether it is firmly grounded in public opinion.

While these are serious matters for serious consideration, the Putney Debates 2017 focused on the direct and immediate consequences of the referendum. One point to note is that the referendum on membership of the EU was not the outcome of popular agitation; it was imposed on the people by the executive and Parliament for reasons other than the common good or the public interest. However, the source of the initiative perhaps does not now matter; it may have been just the spark to ignite a mounting bonfire, which would have ignited anyhow, and which, once in flame, would be hard to quench. Whether there is popular demand for the use of the instrument of referendums to decide major matters of government in the future, we do not know. Caution before leaping to wild and dramatic conclusions is advised.

More troubling than the unknown opinions of the people are those of parliamentarians and their supporters. The referendum was introduced by Act of Parliament without prior explanation, justification or public discussion, and with no guidance as to its status, the Act stating simply: there shall be a referendum! The most troubling of all is that members of the House of Commons should then regard the outcome of the referendum as binding on them, even though the majority consider the outcome contrary to the good of the nation, the common good, the public interest. The conventional constitutional approach should have been to regard the referendum as an indication of opinion (of those voting), as a matter to be given due weight in deciding on the best course of action in the national interest. The abdication of that historic responsibility is one core constitutional concern. We do not know whether Parliament's abdication of responsibility to the popular voice is an isolated incident, after which conventional principles will prevail, or whether it signals a constitutional change for the future.

It is the future that matters, however one views the referendum and its constitutional standing. One issue will be whether, between Parliament and the people, a fresh settlement ought to be agreed, whether the eighteenth-century definition of relations between people and Parliament should be reconsidered. Although that goes beyond the scope of the Putney Debates 2017, a few comments are offered.

IV

The first point to note is that the sovereignty of Parliament, the core of the settlement, was invented by Parliament, with the support of powerful apologists such as William Blackstone, to deal with the growing demands by the people for more involvement in, and influence over, the course of government.

How to contain the people's demands was the social and political problem of the time, to which parliamentary sovereignty was the solution. According to the doctrine, Parliament represents the people, but in a particular sense of representation: it embodies the people, so that, when Parliament is assembled, the people are there assembled. The actions of Parliament are then the actions of the people; the sovereignty of Parliament is the sovereignty of the people. Merging the two, Parliament and the people, is essential to the concept. Parliament acts as if it were the people and does so in the name of the people.

The connection between Parliament and this abstract sense of the people is often overlooked, although it is an essential part of the doctrine of parliamentary sovereignty, and the justification. If Parliament's actions are the actions of the people, as it claims, and because constitutional authority derives ultimately from the people, then the actions of Parliament, by definition, are authoritative. The concept of sovereignty, when expressed in this way, has the further consequence of leaving no constitutional role for the real people. The people cannot be both embodied in Parliament and yet exist *constitutionally* outside Parliament. Although the concept of parliamentary sovereignty is based on a fiction, an artifice, a device invented by Parliament for its own ends, it has provided the framework, over more than two centuries, for reasonably effective government in which the people have acquiesced.

That parliamentary sovereignty should provide the resolution of the constitutional and political upheavals of the eighteenth century was neither predictable nor inevitable; nor is the solution timeless. The debates in Parliament and outside could have taken a different course, as many urged, and ended differently. But for the dark and baleful shadow of the French Revolution, a settlement more favourable to the people might have emerged. The time might now be right to reconsider that resolution; to reconsider how parliamentary sovereignty could be softened and modified to allow the people, the real people, a fuller constitutional engagement in the affairs of government, in its scrutiny and its accountability. The referendum is one such way, although questions as to when it should suitably be used, and under what conditions, need considered answers. Nor should other ways of involving the people, besides the referendum, be overlooked, a matter on which we could learn from the experience of other constitutions.

V

For the second point, we should ask whether the very notion of 'sovereignty' has outlived its usefulness. Whether, indeed, it clarifies the issues or obscures them? The sovereignty of Parliament is embedded in the constitutional consciousness of the British people, or sections of it, so that any revision would encounter stiff opposition. It is, nevertheless, an odd notion fusing two separate ideas: one is the sense of a sovereign nation, the other the institutional arrangements for governing within a nation. In its classic, historical sense, sovereignty applies to a nation in its relations with other nations; it is out of place in designating as sovereign one or other institution of government.

A sovereign nation is separate and independent from other nations and organizations, such as the church; it is self-governing and in charge of its own affairs. Within a sovereign nation, the authority to act as the nation, to direct its affairs externally and to govern internally, has to be vested in human institutions, such as the Parliament, the executive and the courts. How authority is divided and allocated is a matter of constitutional design, and should be reviewed from time to time. The division of authority among Parliament, the executive and the courts was considered during the course of the Putney Debates 2017. Opinions differ as to the exact lines of division among them, but only at the margins, and no case was made for change.

The point for our present purposes is that the division of authority within a constitutional order, which varies from one order to another, has nothing to do with the concept of sovereignty in its classic sense. In consolidating its authority as the supreme lawmaker, Parliament in the eighteenth century fused, or, more accurately, confused, the sovereignty of the nation with the scope of its authority. Those who now say the courts are sovereign, since they have the final say on certain matters of interpretation, make the same error and misuse the concept. The same confusion is apparent in calls for sovereignty of the people. The people are supreme, in the sense that the constitutional order depends on their acceptance; they can even be considered sovereign in the sense of constituting the nation, an idea expressed in those texts that begin *We the People*.

But, however expressed, nothing follows as to their engagement in the affairs of government. Whether their role should be changed or augmented is a matter to be settled according to several factors: the need for good and effective government guided by the principles and values of democracy and liberty, respect for rights, the rule of law and whatever else is considered relevant. These are the matters that guide the design of constitutions, the results of which are usually temporary and contingent (with some exceptions), leaving it open for future generations to make adjustments according to circumstance and opinion. The UK is no different, and should learn from both its own history and the experience of others in considering whether the established constitutional arrangements are fit for contemporary conditions and live up to the expectations of the people. In answering those questions, the concept of sovereignty is a distraction and ought have no place.

In understanding the logic of sovereignty and its place in the constitution, we could learn from other constitutional orders. The Constitution of the Republic of Turkey, while not perhaps the obvious point of reference, on this matter is clear and accurate: the people are the *source* of sovereignty; *sovereignty* is vested in the nation; the *exercise* of sovereignty is entrusted to the institutions of government. The issue in the UK concerns sovereignty only in the third sense: the exercise of authority within the constitution. It involves neither the sovereignty of the nation nor the source of sovereignty. Questions about such matters as the relationship between the people and Parliament, the scope of judicial authority, the powers of the executive, are questions about the exercise of authority. They should be analysed and discussed in step with the principles and values of the society, taking account of the currents of opinion within society, and guided by the need for effective government. That is the path to constitutional construction and review, unobstructed by claims about sovereignty.

VI

A third and final comment links the relationship between the people and Parliament to the wider question of restrictions on Parliament, restrictions that would normally be stated in a written constitutional text. The absence of a written text is sometimes seen as a weakness of the constitutional order of the UK, a subject that arose during the Putney Debates.

As a member of the EU, the UK is subject to European law and to the jurisdiction of the European Court of Justice. Both place restrictions on the authority of Parliament: it must act within the standards set by the institutions of the EU and, in case of dispute, is under the jurisdiction of the Court of Justice. Just how extensive and effective such restrictions are, is a matter for empirical research that has yet to be undertaken. To some, the restrictions are serious enough to provoke one of the battle cries for leaving the Union. Parliament will then be unrestrained constitutionally in the exercise of its lawmaking authority. And since Parliament means, effectively, the House of Commons, where the lords are minor irritants and the monarch a splendid ornament, the result is that, after leaving the EU, the House of Commons will exercise its lawmaking power without constitutional restraints, other than those imposed by the European Convention on Human Rights. Some will greet this as a return to the long-established and correct constitutional order.

But again, we should learn from history. At the time Parliament established itself as the supreme lawmaking authority, the two other parts, the House of Lords and the monarch, exerted real checks and constraints on the powers of the Commons. It was a *balanced constitution*, a term commonly used to signify the powers of each branch and the effect of each on the others. Hume praised the constitution as near perfect because it was a balanced constitution. As the powers of the monarch and the lords have shrunk, those of the Commons have grown, to the point where its powers became constitutionally unrestricted. Far from being a balanced constitution, the position on leaving the EU will be an all-powerful House of Commons. To talk of an elective dictatorship is an exaggeration, but the case for a rebalancing of the constitution, and its entrenchment in a text, is surely strong. Just how that could be brought about, however, is hard to imagine, in the absence of an initiative from the executive or the Commons, which is unlikely since the self-interest of both are best served by the status quo.

VII

In the final session of the Debates, the future of the liberal constitution was considered. While the exact nature of a 'liberal constitution' is open to opinion, respect for liberty is central to our constitution. Britain indeed is the home of political liberty, of the basic idea that the constitution should protect the citizens' liberty to live their lives as they wish, subject to the limits necessary for a coordinated society. How the limits are defined varies from one society to another, but the common feature of the constitutions of European nations is the commitment to liberty and the principles that follow from it.

The constitutional culture referred to as the liberal constitution is now under attack. It is cast by some as the work of elite groups to protect their own interests and to impede the progress of democracy. Now it is true that the constitutional protection of rights and liberties is a constraint on the democratic process. The question, then, is whether the rights and liberties of contemporary constitutions, whether written or not, are of passing value, to be replaced in time by other values: stronger government, more popular involvement, firmer commitment to social solidarity, for instance. While values such as these have a rightful place in the constitution, they should not blind us to the enduring importance of the values of a liberal constitution: respect for rights, free speech, due process and the rule of law. These are surely neither passing nor negotiable; they are the values fought for over centuries in the face of resistance. To cast them aside in the name of popular democracy or social solidarity or strong government would be to reverse the hard-won victories of constitutionalism. And it may be that the best form of protection in the UK is to entrench them in a written constitution. That will be the 'matter of high concernment' for the future.

Index